Companion Book

of

Catholic Days

A Guide to Feasts, Saints,
Holy Days, and Seasons

KAREN EDMISTEN

Published by The Word Among Us Press
7115 Guilford Drive, Suite 100
Frederick, Maryland 21704
wau.org

25 24 23 22 21   1 2 3 4 5

ISBN: 978-1-59325-602-9
eISBN: 978-1-59325-603-6

Design by Suzanne Earl

Made and printed in the United States of America

Library of Congress Control Number: 2021922990

Contents

Introduction

I remember a time when I didn't know what the words "liturgical" and "liturgy" meant.

I grew up in a family that was somewhere on the agnostic-to-atheist continuum. We had no hostility to faith; it just wasn't part of our life as a family. I was firmly in the atheist camp by the time I was in college, but for a variety of reasons, I began to question everything.

Eventually, I started attending a Christian church and discovered that I needed to learn an entirely new vocabulary. The language of religion was novel and sometimes confusing. I was baptized at the age of thirty, and I spent the next five years looking for the right church: not merely a landing spot that "felt right" to me; no, I was on a hunt for Truth. As uncomfortable as it initially made me, that hunt had me repeatedly circling back to the Catholic Church.

Catholicism certainly has its own lexicon. It is a faith of liturgy, formal worship, and liturgical language. For all of my initial confusion, the definition of liturgy is fairly straightforward.

Liturgy refers to the Church's official public worship, such as the Holy Sacrifice of the Mass (the Eucharistic liturgy); all the other sacraments; and the Liturgy of the Hours (the Divine Office), the official set of prayers prayed daily by all priests, certain other religious, and increasingly by laypeople. In other words, we have a formal way of doing things. Structure, rules, and guidelines apply, which also, ironically, free us from sifting through a thousand other options and ideas for prayer and worship.

If liturgy is the entire body of our public worship, the liturgical year is the spine that holds the body upright. The Church structures and formalizes our worship, and the result is a liturgical calendar that we can turn to, depend on, and follow. It's like a living, breathing guidebook that takes our hand and shows us the sights. And it's not just for public worship. We the laity are encouraged to live out the liturgical year in our homes, our "domestic churches" (*Lumen Gentium*, 11).

The Church calendar begins with Advent, a time of watching, waiting, and reflecting on the birth of Jesus and his Second Coming. Advent is followed by the Christmas season, and then we enter Ordinary Time, which is defined mostly by what it is not: Ordinary Time is the part of the year that is not Advent, Christmas, Lent, or Easter. "Ordinary" (for "ordered," or numbered) is a time that is oriented toward the everydayness of our Christian lives. Large chunks of the year are observed as Ordinary Time, but there's nothing ordinary about the many saints and holy, historical events whose feast days are observed throughout those months.

I grew up with chocolate on Valentine's Day, Easter egg hunts, and Santa Claus on Christmas Eve. My mother decorated our house for holidays, and we made a big deal of the celebrations we loved. Though our celebrations were entirely secular, my family elevated certain days to a higher level.

As a newly Catholic mom, I embraced the liturgical year with gusto. This former atheist found enormous joy in the rhythms of the liturgical calendar. I introduced my daughters to the saints through books, beautiful art, craft projects, and baking. We celebrated St. Nicholas Eve and his feast day, made scrumptious St. Lucia bread every December, created a "Lamb of God countdown calendar" for Lent, and made even tiny Lenten sacrifices tangible by throwing a dry bean in a jar to represent each act. And of course, on Easter morning, my daughters were delighted to find that those old dry beans had magically turned into M&M's.

As my children learned about the liturgical year through our activities, I immersed myself further in it too. What was once strange and incomprehensible to me became my rhythm of life. I still had a calendar on the wall that ran from January to December, but I also kept a calendar in my head that ran from Advent to Advent. The Church calendar, with its structure, rules, and guidelines became my true calendar, my anchor, my joy, and the blueprint for my life.

This blueprint and these rhythms enriched my personal spirituality and my relationship with God. Throughout the year—as I learned about and was encouraged by the saints, followed feasts and fasts, investigated the Liturgy of the Hours, and offered up a penance every Friday in commemoration of

Jesus' sacrifice for me—I grew closer to the Lord. I felt more directly in touch with him because I was in touch with his whole family, the communion of saints.

And that's the focus in these pages. As fun and valuable as it is to share the liturgical year with one's family, this book is about *you* and *your relationship* with the Lord, a relationship that has the power and potential to grow more expansive as you connect with him through the Church, her rhythms, and the many celebrations and solemn observances she offers us.

How humbling it was to write this book, to try to cram so many riches into a modest container that can't begin to hold everything worth sharing! This book is not meant to be a comprehensive primer on the liturgical year. I couldn't do justice to the many incredible, inspiring saints I highlighted, and there are so many more I would have loved to include. I could write for years and still not cover every nourishing, edifying feast day. But if I can share a tantalizing taste of the vast feast that is the Catholic liturgical year, I will be grateful to have sat down with you for a time.

Won't you join me at the table?

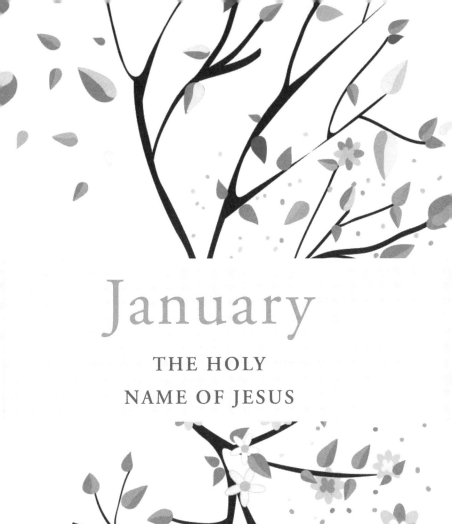

January

THE HOLY
NAME OF JESUS

Happy New Year! Our new year—the liturgical year—actually kicks off at the beginning of Advent, but we live in the world of the Gregorian calendar too, so why not embrace every chance we have for a fresh start? The new liturgical year, packed with feasts, and a fresh calendar year, bursting with promise, offer opportunities to think, reflect, grow, and celebrate. So let's get started—one month, one liturgical season, and one moment for yourself at a time.

January is brimming with possibilities. This month we'll ponder Mary's yes to God, speak the name of Jesus with tenderness, rejoice at epiphanies, fondly look back on our Baptisms, and spend time with a few inspiring and saintly friends.

Get your pen ready to mark favorites, ideas, and inspirations, because the January post-Christmas blahs don't have to be a thing. The liturgical calendar is here to revive us.

Pray

Lord, help me always celebrate, revere, and respect the name of Jesus, never letting it escape my lips without regard for its holiness and meaning. Remind me that a name is not merely a label but the essence of a person, and the holy name of Jesus is a sacramental and a prayer.

Liturgical color

White in the Christmas season
Green when Ordinary Time begins at the end of the Christmas season, after the Baptism of the Lord

A Peek into January's Possibilities

JANUARY 1
Solemnity of Mary, the Holy Mother of God (Holy Day of Obligation)

JANUARY 3
Feast of the Most Holy Name of Jesus

JANUARY 4
Memorial of St. Elizabeth Ann Seton

JANUARY 6 (OR THE SUNDAY BETWEEN JANUARY 2 AND JANUARY 8)
Solemnity of the Epiphany

SUNDAY AFTER JANUARY 6
Solemnity of the Baptism of the Lord

JANUARY 22
Day of Prayer for the Unborn

JANUARY 24
Memorial of St. Francis de Sales

JANUARY 25
Feast of the Conversion of St. Paul the Apostle

JANUARY 27
Optional Memorial of St. Angela Merici

January 1

SOLEMNITY OF MARY, HOLY MOTHER OF GOD

Connect

Why are there *so many* Marian feast days? We celebrate the Annunciation, the Assumption of Mary, the Immaculate Conception, as well as many other events in her life, such as the Visitation of Mary to Elizabeth. There's a kaleidoscope of titles for Mary too: "Comfort of Christians," "Help to the Helpless," "Ark of the Covenant," and "Mother of Divine Love." Sometimes it seems as if Mary is everywhere and has a million responsibilities to uphold.

Sound familiar? So much to do and so little time.

With so many Marian feasts to observe and titles to ponder, why should we pay attention to this one in particular? This observance might sometimes feel like an obligation that makes an already busy holiday week even more hectic. But there are powerful underpinnings for this solemnity and compelling reasons to celebrate.

January 1 is the eighth day in the Octave of Christmas. The Church officially sets aside eight days, from December 25 to January 1, to celebrate Christ's birth. The feast is so big that we need a weeklong party! The formal liturgical name for January 1 is the Octave Day of Christmas, Solemnity of Mary, the Holy Mother of God.

As with all Marian feast days, this one is actually all about Jesus. It's the culminating day of the extended celebration of our King's birth. It's also an opportunity to reflect on Mary's fiat, her yes to bringing Christ incarnate into the world. As St. Ambrose said, "The first thing which kindles ardor in learning is the greatness of the teacher. What is greater than the Mother of God? What more glorious than she whom Glory Itself chose?"[1]

The world is bustling with New Year's Eve revelry, New Year's Day resolutions, and fresh starts. As you head to Mass to celebrate the Mother of God, you can renew your spiritual resolutions and pray for a fresh start too—whatever that looks like for you.

To Ponder or Do

- Mary shows us what it means to put our lives in God's hands. I can't think of a better New Year's resolution than asking God to help me live as Mary did: to say yes to what he'll ask of me over the next twelve months. Each person's yes will look different, but one fact remains: God is calling me to do, say, pray, or change something. What is it?

- This year consider Mary from a new angle. Have you ever viewed obedience as weakness? Consider the courage it took for Mary to live out her yes to God. She risked ridicule, shunning, abandonment, and the shattering of dreams she might have had for a normal life. Yet she knew that her encounter with the angel Gabriel heralded something sublime and profound. There was no dismissing it. A decision had to be made.

  If you've ever considered Mary to be so perfect that her yes didn't really indicate a free choice, remind yourself that she had just as much freedom as we do. And because her free will wasn't tarnished by original sin, her choices were clearer to her than ours are to us. Her thinking wasn't clouded by the selfishness we battle, but that doesn't negate her decisions. She still had to live with the consequences of every yes and no, just as we do.

- Think about an area in which you struggle to say yes to God. Is there a sin that keeps you attached to a no? You may or may not be the New Year's resolution type, but this year, consider one resolution: to pray about the consequences of every yes and every no in your life.

Pray

As you embark on the new year, ask for Mary's intercession using the *Memorare*. Pray it whenever you feel the need for an ally. It's short and powerful. But don't forget: you can always pray even shorter prayers, such as these:

"Blessed Mother, pray for me."
"Mary, help me out here!"
"Mother Mary, this day is awful. Please pray *now*!"

She gets it.

The Memorare

Remember, O most gracious Virgin Mary,
that never was it known
that anyone who fled to thy protection,
implored thy help,
or sought thy intercession
was left unaided.
Inspired by this confidence
I fly unto thee,
O Virgin of virgins, my Mother.
To thee do I come,
before thee I stand,
sinful and sorrowful.
O Mother of the Word Incarnate,

despite not my petitions,
but in thy mercy hear and answer me.
Amen.

January 3

THE MOST HOLY NAME OF JESUS

Connect

What's in a name? Names are interesting things. Of course, there are myriad practical considerations and reasons for having names: so that we know what to call someone, how to get their attention, what to print on their passport or scribble on their name tag at a conference. But names have deeper meanings.

In the Bible, a name can signify a person's mission: a name change can indicate that someone is being asked to take on a new role. Abram became Abraham, Sarai became Sarah, and Jacob became Israel. Isaiah the prophet foretold the name of Jesus:

For a child is born to us, a son is given to us;
upon his shoulder dominion rests.

They name him Wonder-Counselor, God-Hero,
Father-Forever, Prince of Peace. (Isaiah 9:5)

And long before the time of Isaiah, God gave Adam the responsibility of naming all the animals (see Genesis 2:19-20).

To bestow a name is to establish a relationship. Names have power! They connect us.

To Ponder or Do

- What does it look like to celebrate the Most Holy Name of Jesus? The goal is to connect to the meaning, power, and grandeur of his name and to acknowledge the lordship of the divine being behind the name. The second commandment exhorts us to never use the Lord's name in vain but rather to venerate, respect, and cherish it. It's *that* important.

- When you consider the names of people special to you—your grandmother, your child, your best friend, your spouse—you consider the core identity of that person. You feel connected. Consider how much more precious the name of Jesus is and how we're called to connect deeply with his identity and his place in our lives. Try praying simply with the name of Jesus: "Jesus, be with me," "Jesus, mercy," "Jesus, come to us."

- Have you ever noticed at Mass that many times when a priest speaks the name of Jesus, he bows his head? Pope Gregory X initiated this gesture in the thirteenth century, to recall Philippians 2:10, that "at the name of Jesus every knee should bend." The gesture isn't just for priests. The laity can also show their reverence and love for our Lord's name with a simple bow of the head each time his name is mentioned.

What's in a name? If it's the holy name of Jesus, *everything*.

Pray

There's nothing like a litany to help us slow down and pray with patience and intention. Litanies are long and repetitive, so pray this one when you have time to settle in and savor it. It's easy to find it online, but here's how it begins:

Litany of the Holy Name of Jesus

Lord, have mercy. *Lord, have mercy.*
Christ, have mercy. *Christ, have mercy.*
Lord, have mercy. *Lord, have mercy.*
Jesus, hear us. *Jesus, hear us.*
Jesus, graciously hear us. *Jesus, graciously hear us.*

God, the Father of Heaven, *have mercy on us.*
God the Son, Redeemer of the world, *have mercy on us.*
God, the Holy Spirit, *have mercy on us.*

Holy Trinity, one God, *have mercy on us.*
Jesus, Son of the living God, *have mercy on us.*
Jesus, splendor of the Father, *have mercy on us.*
Jesus, brightness of eternal Light, *have mercy on us.*
Jesus, king of Glory, *have mercy on us.*

January 4

ST. ELIZABETH ANN SETON

(1774–1821)

*Wife, mother, religious; patron of widows, of those with
in-law problems, against the death of children and parents,
and of those ridiculed for their faith.*

Elizabeth Ann Bayley Seton was the first American-born
saint canonized by the Catholic Church. She was born
into an Episcopalian family. Her mother died when Elizabeth
was just three years old. After a lonely childhood, in 1794
Elizabeth married William Seton. They had five children and
a happy marriage, albeit a tragically short one. William died
of tuberculosis in 1803 during a trip to Italy meant to boost
his ailing health.

Influenced by the beauty of Catholicism and the piety of
her Catholic friends in Italy, Elizabeth converted when she
returned home. In response to anti-Catholic prejudice rampant

in America, she opened a school in Maryland, setting the stage for the Catholic school system in the United States. She allowed children from underprivileged families to attend free. She expanded her work, took religious vows, and founded the Sisters of Charity of St. Joseph, the first order for religious women founded in America.

Elizabeth was no stranger to devastating loss, enduring the deaths of her husband, mother, sister, and two young daughters. She must have been tempted to give up numerous times, but the hundreds of letters that she left behind reveal a steadfast woman who pushed on, always with hope. She is a model of trust in God.

- Has an experience of loss ever threatened to derail you? How did you get back on track? Ask Elizabeth Seton to intercede for you whenever you feel overwhelmed.

Confiding hope and consoling peace have attended my way through storms and dangers that must have terrified a soul whose rock is not Christ.

—St. Elizabeth Ann Seton[2]

PILGRIMAGE ALERT

Emmitsburg, Maryland, is home to the Shrine of St. Elizabeth Ann Seton, where her remains are entombed. You can tour the grounds and the historic homes where Elizabeth lived and worked. Visit setonshrine.org to learn more.

If you're in New York City, visit the Seton Shrine at Our Lady of the Rosary Church (spcolr.org/st-seton-shrine-1).

January 6

SOLEMNITY OF THE EPIPHANY

Connect

The Epiphany celebrates the visit of the Magi, traditionally referred to as the three kings, to the infant Christ Child. The feast is typically observed on January 6, but in the United States, the observance is on the Sunday between January 2 and 8.

The word "epiphany" means "manifestation." On this feast, we celebrate the fact that the Messiah of Israel was made manifest not only to the Jews but to the Gentiles, in the persons of the wise men from the East. In other words, the universal Messiah has arrived—for *everyone*!

When we envision the Magi visiting the Holy Family, do we imagine a serene scene of distant royalty coming to town to pay respects and to offer odd congratulatory gifts? Or do we look beyond this pretty picture and grasp the earthshaking news that rocked the Magi's world? The wise men represented pagan traditions, and yet they *fell down and worshipped* as

Lord of the universe the Jewish son of a young woman and a common carpenter. Matthew 2:11-12 tells us,

> They prostrated themselves and did him homage. Then they opened their treasures and offered him gifts of gold, frankincense, and myrrh. And having been warned in a dream not to return to Herod, they departed for their country by another way.

To Ponder or Do

- In common vocabulary, we use the word "epiphany" to speak of a moment of enlightenment, a realization, or an illumination. Was there one moment in your life when you first genuinely acknowledged Jesus as Lord of the universe? As *your* Lord? Or are you still waiting for or longing for your own epiphany? What's at stake for you as you acknowledge Jesus' place in your life?

- If you're looking for fresh ways to celebrate the Epiphany, consider exchanging Epiphany gifts with family members or a friend, to emphasize the power of this feast. If you want to go big, plan a Twelfth Night party. Remind friends and family that the Christmas season didn't end after Christmas Day: the Twelve Days of Christmas are alive and well!

  In high school, my best friend invited me to his family's Twelfth Night party. I was surprised to discover that Catholics were so good at spreading joy. It turned out to be a wonderful bit of stealth evangelism on the part of my friend's family.

- If you have children, a traditional activity is to make an Epiphany or king's cake and hide a coin or trinket inside. The child who finds the treasure is king or queen for the day. This celebration can be as easy or elaborate as you like: use anything from store-bought cupcakes to a homemade treat decorated with jewels—your kids' favorite candy—to look like a crown.

  Don't want or need the sugar? Make paper crowns with the kids. Everyone can be king or queen for the day. Congratulate one another for recognizing the kingship of Christ.

Pray

Open my eyes, Lord, that I may see my King.
Open my ears, Lord, that I may hear your word and apply it to my life.
Open my mouth, Lord, that I may proclaim your love in a harsh world.
Open my mind, heart, and soul, Lord, that I may worship you freely, fully, and without hesitation, and share your all-encompassing love with others.

Sunday after Epiphany

SOLEMNITY OF THE BAPTISM OF THE LORD

Connect

Every year since 1981, the pope has baptized infants at the Vatican on the Solemnity of the Baptism of the Lord. In his Angelus address on January 12, 2020, after baptizing thirty-two babies, Pope Francis said, of Jesus and his Baptism, that Jesus has

> the attitude of meekness—the attitude of simplicity, of respect, of moderation, and of hiddenness that is still asked today of the Lord's disciples. How many—it is sad to say—how many of the Lord's disciples boast that they are disciples of the Lord. Those who boast are not good disciples of the Lord.

Pope Francis continued:

> The good disciple is humble, meek, one who does good unobtrusively. In missionary work, the Christian community is called

to approach others always offering and not imposing, bearing witness, sharing the concrete life of the people.[3]

To Ponder or Do

- Baptism sets in motion the call to mission and evangelization. It's easy to interpret that as a daunting task in a huge broken world. But Jesus doesn't expect us to save the world. He asks us only to look at our corner of it.

- We can start with our friends and family. Even more simply, we can start by finding out more about our own Baptism. Do you know when you were baptized? At the 2020 Baptism event in the Vatican, Pope Francis assigned some "homework." He asked those present to find out the date of their Baptism and celebrate that date every year. If that indeed feels like homework and you're thinking, "No, thank you!" but you know you were baptized as an infant, just grab a day within a month of your birthday, and use that as your celebration day.

  When my daughters were growing up, we enjoyed having extra celebrations on the calendar. Everyone knew that a baptismal day was a treat day. If I felt like baking, we might have brownies or chocolate chip cookies. In busier times, I simply pulled someone's favorite candy bar from my pantry stash. We didn't make it complicated or labor intensive; we just enjoyed recalling and celebrating the days we became children of God.

- If you were baptized as an adult, you probably know the date. Be sure to celebrate your day too! Observances like these can even lead to casual opportunities for sharing the faith. If you mention to a friend that you're indulging in chocolate because it's your baptismal birthday, it might spark an interesting conversation.

  As Pope Paul VI said in his apostolic exhortation *Evangelii Nuntiandi*, the world needs Christians with "an interior enthusiasm that nobody and nothing can quench." He continued,

And may the world of our time, which is searching, sometimes with anguish, sometimes with hope, be enabled to receive the Good News not from evangelizers who are dejected, discouraged, impatient, or anxious, but from ministers of the Gospel whose lives glow with fervor, who have first received the joy of Christ.[4]

Pray

Lord, thank you for the gift of my Baptism. Help me see my call to be light in the world as a series of simple steps and loving actions rather than as an overwhelming responsibility that is beyond me. Help me start with the people nearest me, by offering simple thanksgiving for the gift of this sacrament.

Ordinary Time Alert

After celebrating the Baptism of the Lord, we enter into Ordinary Time.

"Ordinary Time" refers to the days of the liturgical calendar that are "ordered," or numbered, outside of the preparatory seasons of Advent and Lent and the grand seasons of celebration, Christmas and Easter. It's tempting to think of Ordinary Time as the humdrum, routine days that are of less importance, but Mother Church is marvelous about adjusting our perspective. There are still feasts to indulge in and saints to laud and honor in the days before Lent. The liturgical calendar, even in its simple, ordered progression, reminds us that there is always something meaningful to focus on in a life of faith.

With Christmas in the past and weeks before Lent begins, consider doing something to honor the liturgical color associated with Ordinary Time. Green is the color of fresh new growth, so perhaps you can buy a new plant. If you're like me, with a tendency to wilt all indoor greenery, consider some fake greenery.

Or you could forgo the plant and remind yourself of Ordinary Time with a simple prayer list: use green ink to copy a prayer, write a list of petitions, or compile the names of those you want to pray for during this season. Mount the list on green card stock or construction paper. The idea is to create a visual reminder and a nod to the liturgical season we're living in.

January 22

DAY OF PRAYER
FOR THE UNBORN

Today, in addition to our prayers for unborn children and for an end to the misery and devastation of abortion, let's pray for all women who have had abortions, for women who at this very moment may be considering abortion as their only option, and for fathers who have participated in or advocated for this tragic decision. Pray that all receive the support, tools, and practical and spiritual assistance that will allow them to move away from the fear, coercion, and desperation that drive people to this sad and lonely choice. Pray that all men and women who are contemplating or have had abortions or have played a part in seeking abortions can experience the love and forgiveness of Christ, who awaits them with open arms.

January 24

ST. FRANCIS DE SALES
(1567–1622)

Priest, bishop, Doctor of the Church; patron of writers, editors, journalists, the Catholic press, and the deaf

St. Francis de Sales is the friend we all need, the one we'd love to meet for coffee and good conversation. I wouldn't mind finding him in the confessional either, as he was known as something of a genius there. Universally acknowledged as a lovable man, he believed that each and every one of us is capable of holiness, a teaching that was revolutionary in his time.

This saint famously had a deep spiritual friendship with St. Jane Frances de Chantal, becoming her spiritual director and pursuing a lengthy, ongoing correspondence with her. His mentoring friendship led them to cofound the Order of the Visitation, a religious order for women who were unable to undertake the rigors of many religious orders of the time.

Francis is the saint many turn to for practical help, down-to-earth reassurance, and profound, uncomplicated wisdom. His books—*Introduction to the Devout Life*, *Treatise on the Love of God*, and others—are like drinks of cool, clean water for a parched throat. He is perpetually both encouraging and consoling.

- Have you found a genius confessor? The priest in the confessional doesn't have to be perfect to be *in persona Christi* for you. Whether he offers transcendent spiritual advice or mutters his way through the words of absolution, he is acting as Christ for you, and you are forgiven. Have you had a chance to go to Confession lately?

Have patience with all things, but chiefly have patience with yourself. Do not lose courage in considering your own imperfections, but instead set about remedying them—every day begin the task anew.

—St. Francis de Sales[5]

January 25

FEAST OF THE CONVERSION OF ST. PAUL

Connect

Is St. Paul the definitive convert? His story certainly gives us pause. Saul was a fanatic anti-Christian and persecutor of the followers of Christ, yet after a genuine encounter with Jesus on the road to Damascus, he was transformed (see Acts 9 for the riveting story of his conversion). He dropped everything, blew off his old life, and followed the Lord. His conversion was obvious from every angle.

Not all conversions will be so dramatic or visible. Once, after a youth group leader had asked kids to share the moment they knew God was real, my daughter came home and said, "I don't have one of those exciting, dramatic stories. I've just always known he was there. He's *always* been there for me."

Such quiet, steadfast faith is as real, sturdy, and strong as the kind of faith that comes from a lightning-bolt moment. Never discount or diminish such abiding faith, and offer gratitude whenever you see it in your kids or in anyone who has quietly maintained faith over the course of a lifetime.

To Ponder or Do

- No matter when we came to God—baptized as an infant or as an adult or meeting the risen Christ and dropping everything to follow him, as Saul did—we're all called to ongoing conversion. Just as we never stop growing emotionally, the Lord calls us to grow spiritually, to let Jesus change our lives a little more every day.

- Msgr. Robert Hugh Benson, in his book *An Average Man*, said, "There is no happiness in the world comparable to that of the experience known as conversion." [6] How has Jesus changed you? Did you have a road-to-Damascus moment, or has your faith always been there, like a reliable, loving companion on a long, hard trip? If you had to define "conversion" in your faith life, what would you say?

- Read the Acts of the Apostles 9:1-19. In this passage about Paul's conversion, a disciple named Ananias responds to God's call with "Here I am, Lord" (9:10). But then he doubts the instructions the Lord gives him because he knows of Saul's persecutions and evil deeds. God's response is basically "Hey, listen up. I know best." Ananias follows God's instructions and lays hands on Paul. So the next time you feel skeptical about what God seems to be calling you to do, try responding with the prayerful words "Here I am, Lord," and see what happens.

Pray

Lord, I want to follow you without question, but sometimes I doubt your plans. Help me to acknowledge those times you call me and to pray for discernment, clarity, and confirmation. Then help me respond, "Here I am, Lord."

January 27

ST. ANGELA MERICI (1474–1540)

Founder of the Ursulines, an order dedicated to educating girls and young women; patron of the sick, disabled, and those who have lost parents.

St. Angela was born in Desenzano, Italy. After the deaths of her parents, when she was only ten years old, Angela and her sister went to live with an uncle in Salo. Angela's sister died shortly after. When her uncle died, Angela, then twenty years old, moved back to her hometown. Despite the grief and losses she had endured, her faith was strong. She was granted a mystical vision of her sister in heaven, which further strengthened her faith.

Angela developed a strong desire to share the faith, especially with other women. In Desenzano she was disturbed to see the level of ignorance among girls and young women. She started teaching them in her home, and her pioneering, innovative approach to education was infectious and inviting. Other women joined her efforts, gathering and catechizing children in their homes too.

Angela's loosely formed but firmly cemented sisterhood eventually became the Order of Ursulines, after St. Ursula. Little is known about St. Ursula, but legends attest to her fervent piety and martyrdom with a group of other women.

- St. Angela Merici wasn't afraid to shake things up and try new methods in a time when change wasn't the order of the day. Is change easy for you, or do you struggle with it? In matters of flexible religious practice, do you yearn for innovation, or do you like to stick with tried-and-true approaches?

Our Savior says that a good tree, that is, a good heart as well as a soul on fire with charity, can do nothing but good and holy works.

—St. Angela Merici[7]

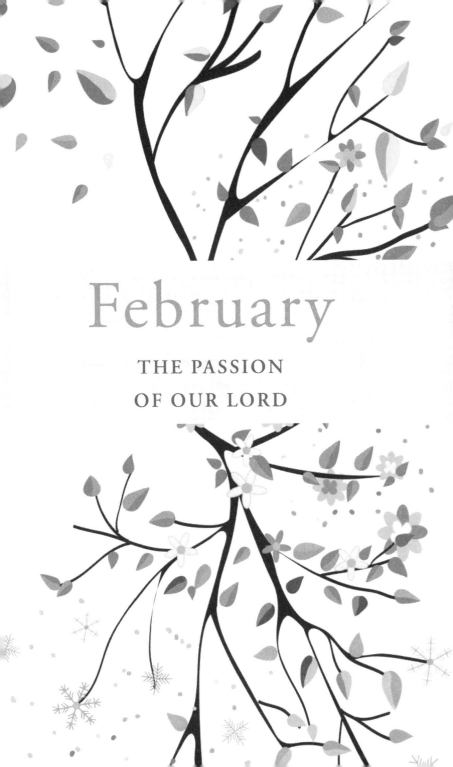

February

THE PASSION
OF OUR LORD

Febuary is predictable in its unpredictability. Groundhog Day highlights the capricious nature of late winter: will the frigid weather continue or make an early exit? Lent also seems capricious in its arrival. Will Ash Wednesday fall in February, setting up the dreaded conflict with Valentine's Day chocolate? Or will Lent arrive later, perhaps not showing up until March 10, the latest possible date for that liturgical marker to make its appearance?

The earliest date on which Lent can fall is February 4, which feels far too soon after our January return to Ordinary Time. That jolting schedule won't happen again until the year 2285. Lent most commonly begins in mid to late February or the earliest days of March.

Wherever Lent falls this year, February offers us plenty of potential to dive into the liturgical calendar as we observe Candlemas and spend time with inspiring saintly witnesses.

Pray

Lord, as we near the season of Lent and our annual deepened contemplation of your passion, help me remember, each and every day, what you did for me. I want your passion to be the central passion of my life.

Liturgical Color

Green when in Ordinary Time
Purple during Lent

A Peek into February's Possibilities

FEBRUARY 1
Optional Memorial of St. Brigid

FEBRUARY 2
Feast of the Presentation of the Lord, Candlemas

FEBRUARY 3
Optional Memorial of St. Blaise

FEBRUARY 8
Optional Memorial of St. Josephine Bakhita

FEBRUARY 10
Memorial of St. Scholastica

FEBRUARY 22
Feast of the Chair of St. Peter

FEBRUARY 27
Optional Memorial of St. Gregory of Narek

February 1

ST. BRIGID OF IRELAND
(C. 450–524)

Founder of the first convent in Ireland; patron of Ireland (with St. Patrick and St. Columba), babies, dairy workers, travelers, students, and the printing press

Not a great deal is known about Brigid beyond numerous legends, but all accounts agree on her extravagant charity and cheerfulness. When she was young, she purportedly got into trouble often for giving food to the poor.

Brigid founded the first convent of nuns in Ireland, at Kildare, which means "Church of the Oak." The convent became a double monastery, housing separately both nuns and monks.

Brigid's influence in spreading Catholicism throughout Ireland is undisputed, and it's generally accepted that she was a friend of St. Patrick. It's believed that her remains lie next to those of St. Patrick and St. Columba on the grounds of Down Cathedral in Downpatrick, Northern Ireland.

- Brigid was said to be extravagant in her generosity and care for others. Spiritual extravagance was the only kind she cared about. Her selflessness is inspiring.

- Is there a material extravagance in your life that you've felt called to leave behind? Trust that God will restore, in unpredictable ways, whatever you give up for his sake. He can help us redefine "extravagance."

I would like an abundance of peace. I would like full vessels of charity. I would like rich treasures of mercy. I would like cheerfulness to preside over all.

—St. Brigid[8]

February 2

FEAST OF THE PRESENTATION OF THE LORD, CANDLEMAS

Connect

Joseph and Mary fulfilled the Mosaic laws of ritual purification when they took Jesus to the temple forty days after his birth and presented him to the Lord. Simeon and Anna, prophets and champions of prayer, immediately recognized Jesus as the Messiah. Simeon's beautiful canticle (see Luke

2:29-32) and his unsettling prophecy to Mary (2:34-35) have been incorporated into the Liturgy of the Hours, the daily prayer of the Church.

Today's Mass includes the blessing of candles for the coming year, thus the name "Candlemas." This practice came about sometime in the fifth century. It wasn't originally connected to the Presentation, yet it seems fitting to align this rite with the Presentation of Jesus, the light of the world. Originally the blessing was for the candles to be used in church, but parishioners also bring candles to Mass that day to have them blessed.

Although we're entering the second month of the year, it still feels like a time for resolutions. In an older version of the liturgical calendar, the Christmas season ended on this feast, rather than in January with the Baptism of the Lord. Why not use today as another opportunity for a fresh start or a recharge, with a nod toward rituals and ceremonies in your life?

As I think about today's feast, I like to consider spiritual practices I approach with a sense of obligation. How can I deepen an area in which I'm just going through the motions?

To Ponder or Do

- When Mary presented her son in the Temple, Simeon told her that "a sword will pierce through your own soul also" (Luke 2:35, RSVCE). We know that, as Mary is giving her son to God at this moment, she will also give her son to God when she is at the foot of the cross. To do what is right, to do what she is called to do, means that she will experience extensive suffering in her life as a mother.

- You don't have to be a mother to know that life involves suffering. Every time we accept a gift from God, we cradle and cherish it, as Mary cradled Jesus; but we know God could ask us to "present" it back to him at any time.

  Remember that this moment was also for Mary's "purification." Granted, the Immaculate Conception didn't have to go through ritual purification in order to be a role model for us. But in doing so, she showed us what purification can mean. Every time we accept a cross, carry it willingly, and offer it to God, we are purified, becoming more who God wants us to be.

- Take some candles to Mass on February 2 and have them blessed. These might be candles that you'll light during mealtimes, during morning or evening prayer time, or simply when you want to be reminded of Jesus, the light of the world.

- Today, when you consider the gifts God has given to you, ask yourself if you have had to surrender any of them. If so, has that loss helped you grow closer to him?

Pray

Simeon's prophecy, known as the Canticle of Simeon, is part of night prayer within the Liturgy of the Hours. It's a short and beautiful reminder of God's saving presence in the world:

> Now, Master, you may let your servant go
>   in peace, according to your word,
> for my eyes have seen your salvation,
>   which you prepared in sight of all the peoples,
> a light for revelation to the Gentiles,
>   and glory for your people Israel. (Luke 2:29-32)

February 3

ST. BLAISE (DIED C. 316)

Bishop, martyr, physician; patron of throat illness, coughs, veterinarians, wool combers, wool weavers, animals

We don't know a lot about St. Blaise; most of what we do know comes from the *Acts of St. Blaise*, written four hundred years after his death. He was a doctor and bishop in Armenia in the fourth century, and he was martyred during the reign of Emperor Licinius.

At some point, on his way to prison or during his imprisonment, Blaise purportedly healed a young boy who was choking on a fishbone. That episode forms the basis of his intercession for those with throat problems, a patronage that has endured. Before he was beheaded, his flesh was torn with wool combs, which led to his patronage of those in the wool trade.

On this feast day, a priest or deacon blesses the throats of the faithful with two candles that have been bound with red ribbon in the form of a cross. The celebrant pronounces the following blessing: "Through the intercession of St. Blaise, bishop and martyr, may God deliver you from every disease of the throat and from every other disease. In the name of the Father, and of the Son, and of the Holy Spirit."

- Stories about St. Blaise's courageous faith and compassionate healing have survived the ages. Even if some stories in the lives of saints are legend, we do know that miracles happen. It seems less important to sift through their veracity than to embrace the fact that examples of miraculous healing can easily be found, even today, and especially in association with saintly intercession.

  Have you ever sought healing intercession from a saint? Have you ever had your throat blessed on St. Blaise's feast day? How have you experienced these opportunities to rely on your friends in the communion of saints?

I see clearly that the thing the church needs most today is the ability to heal wounds and to warm the hearts of the faithful; it needs nearness, proximity.

—Pope Francis [9]

February 8

ST. JOSEPHINE BAKHITA
(1868–1947)

Religious; patron of Sudan and human trafficking survivors

Although she later wrote that the earliest years of her life were happy and carefree, the trauma St. Josephine endured for many years caused her to literally forget who she was: she could not remember her birth name.

Born in the village of Olgossa in southern Sudan, this saint was kidnapped at the age of seven and sold into slavery. While enslaved, she was given the name Bakhita, which means "lucky" or "fortunate." She was bought and sold repeatedly to a series of cruel masters who beat her frequently: one beat her nearly to death when she broke a vase; another had her tattooed according to a ritual that involved well over a hundred cuts on her body and the pouring of salt into the wounds.

An Italian consul, Callisto Legnani, bought Bakhita when she was fifteen. The family treated her kindly, and eventually she accompanied them to Italy, where slavery was in fact illegal. Nevertheless, Bakhita served as a slave to friends of the Legnanis, the Michieli family, caring for their baby, Mimmina.

When the Michielis had to attend to work obligations elsewhere, they left Bakhita and Mimmina in the care of the Canossian Sisters of the Institute of the Catechumens in Venice. There Bakhita came to know and love God. With the help of the sisters, she sought, fought for, and gained her freedom. She was baptized Josephine on January 9, 1890, and in 1896 consecrated herself to the Lord forever as a Canossian sister.

At her canonization Mass on October 1, 2000, Pope John Paul II said,

> In St. Josephine Bakhita we find *a shining advocate of genuine emancipation*. The history of her life inspires not passive acceptance but the firm resolve to work effectively to free girls and women from oppression and violence, and to return them to their dignity in the full exercise of their rights.[10]

St. Josephine Bakhita's last words were "Our Lady! Our Lady!"

- It's painful to imagine all that St. Josephine endured. And yet, having seen and experienced untold horrors, she was able to recognize the beauty of God's work in her life and to embrace the intercession of the Blessed Mother. Today ask St. Josephine to pray for you, and say a prayer for all victims of human trafficking and all those affected by the horrors of enslavement of every kind.

Seeing the sun, the moon and the stars, I said to myself:
Who could be the Master of these beautiful things?
And I felt a great desire to see him, to know him, and
to pay him homage.

—St. Josephine Bakhita [11]

February 10

ST. SCHOLASTICA (C. 480–547)

Religious, the sister of St. Benedict; patron of nuns

Most of what we know about St. Scholastica comes from the *Dialogues* of St. Gregory the Great, who gave us the most famous story of this nun and her brother.

Benedict founded his monastery at Monte Cassino and probably also established the nearby monastery of nuns to which Scholastica, who had vowed herself to God very early in life, belonged. Because women were not allowed to enter the men's monastery, Benedict and Scholastica met once a year at a house a short way from Monte Cassino. There they spent the day "in the praises of God and spiritual talk," which as we see from this story, was clearly a two-way street.[12]

Both Scholastica and Benedict were advanced in years and knew that each annual meeting could be their last. So one year, Scholastica asked Benedict to stay longer and talk through the night. He refused; staying late would violate his monastic rule. At this point, Scholastica bowed her head and prayed.

Suddenly a crashing thunderstorm was upon them, and Benedict could not leave. He admonished his sister for her unfair tactics, and she confidently stated, "I desired you to stay, and you would not hear me; I have desired it of our good Lord, and he has granted my petition."[13]

Scholastica knew how to keep her brother on track. As St. Gregory wrote, "Therefore, as is right, she who loved more, did more."[14] St. Scholastica died three days later.

- It can be easy to become rigid in our practice of the faith, falling into habits that prevent us from living the gospel freely, with compassion for others. When Scholastica begged God to let her brother stay with her, she demonstrated her freedom from such rigidity.

  Have you ever had to perform a rigidity check or remind yourself that, as Scripture says in this regard, the Sabbath was made for us, not the other way around?

The man of God, seeing that he could not, in the midst of such thunder and lightning and great abundance of rain return to his Abbey, began to be heavy and to complain to his sister, saying: "God forgive you, what have you done?" She answered him, "I desired you to stay, and you would not hear me; I have desired it of our good Lord, and he has granted my petition. Therefore if you can now depart, in God's name return to your monastery, and leave me here alone."

— St. Gregory the Great[15]

February 22

FEAST OF THE CHAIR OF ST. PETER, APOSTLE

Connect

The name of today's feast sounds a bit impersonal. Of course, we're not actually celebrating a chair but rather everything that the chair represents: the authority of St. Peter as the first bishop of Rome and therefore our first pope. And yet an actual chair exists and is in St. Peter's Basilica in Rome. The *Catholic Encyclopedia* tells us that in the early Church,

> a chair (*cathedra*) was venerated which the Apostle [Peter] had used as presiding officer of the assembly of the faithful. . . .
>
> . . . According to the examination then made by Padre Garucci and Giovanni Battista de Rossi, the oldest portion . . . is a perfectly plain oaken arm-chair with four legs connected by cross-bars. The wood is much worm-eaten, and pieces have been cut from various spots at different times, evidently for relics. . . . At a later date, perhaps in the ninth century, this famous chair was strengthened by the addition of pieces of acacia wood. The latter wood has inlaid in it a rich ornamentation of ivory.[16]

Why do we celebrate the chair in which Peter sat? First, the Church reminds us of the reality of papal authority. Jesus established the papacy and placed Peter as the first in a long, successive line. Popes are imperfect men, but they are part of a mechanism that Jesus put in motion for perpetuating the Church on earth. That alone is worth celebrating.

Second, this feast reminds us of the power of a sacramental, such as the chair, and of how inseparable we are from a sensory existence. The *Catechism of the Catholic Church* says sacramentals

> are sacred signs which bear a resemblance to the sacraments. They signify effects, particularly of a spiritual nature, which are obtained through the intercession of the Church. By them men are disposed to receive the chief effect of the sacraments, and various occasions in life are rendered holy." (1667)

Sacramentals become "sacred signs," not because the object, such as the chair, is inherently worthy, but because of the Church's intercessory blessing. Sacramentals symbolize holiness, but they also become holy.

It's not the chair the Church asks us to celebrate. Rather, it is the human being who sat in that chair and played a central role in the development of the Church that Jesus gave us. The chair would not have been preserved if St. Peter hadn't sat in it, and Peter would not have occupied it if Jesus hadn't directly and deliberately left us with an earthly leader.

Pondering or looking upon the Chair of St. Peter, then, is like considering a gift from our Lord himself.

To Ponder or Do

- Consider reading the entire entry on the Chair of St. Peter in the *Catholic Encyclopedia*, and search online for pictures.

- Think about what the authority of the papacy or the teaching office of the Church in general has meant to you.

  Recently I was talking to one of my daughters about the various choices people make regarding burial, cremation, and so on. We'd watched a TV show in which a character wanted her ashes scattered in a variety of places. I told my daughter that before I became a Catholic, my opinion on many things bounced around like a pinball, changing daily. Once I became a Catholic, I realized that the Church offered beautiful guidance and teaching on many subjects and provided a grounding viewpoint and lens through which I could see the world.

  In the case of burials, for example, the focus always returned to the dignity of the human person. Suddenly the Church's teachings on burial—or cremation with respectful burial of ashes—made sense to me.

- Is there an area of life in which the culture offers many options, and you aren't sure which one is right? As Catholics, we have freedom in many situations, but in matters of faith and morals, the Church offers the backbone upon which we can build the body of our lives.

If you've never taken time to look at the *Catechism of the Catholic Church*, consider buying a copy and looking up anything you're curious about. You may be surprised at the commonsense teaching. Or you might be startled to learn about an area in which the Church guides you to use your best prudential judgment.

Pray

St. Peter, you were the first pope, a gift to us from our Lord Jesus Christ. Help me remember that Jesus created the office of pope, symbolized by your chair, in order to guide us, lead us, and be with us in a tangible way as we walk on this earth. Pray for us to be faithful witnesses for Jesus every day, and remind me to pray daily for our pope and the burdens and joys of leadership and witness that he carries.

February 27

ST. GREGORY OF NAREK
(C. 950–1003)

Named a Doctor of the Church by Pope Francis in 2015, St. Gregory of Narek was an Armenian monk, mystic, poet, and composer. His *Book of Lamentations*, while not well-known in the United States, is beloved in Armenia. St Gregory called this book an "encyclopedia of prayer for all nations," hoping that his work could reach and speak to people all over the world:

> May this book of prayers I have undertaken to compose with the strength of the Holy Spirit and with a view to the multitudinous needs of all serve for some as heartfelt pleas of intercession and for others as counsel toward virtue that through this book they might constantly appear before you, Great Mercy:
>
> May you heal the souls and wash away the transgressions of those who read this book with pure hearts.[17]

In his book *The Doctor of Mercy: The Sacred Treasures of St. Gregory of Narek*, author and professor Dr. Michael Papazian dubbed Gregory "the Doctor of Mercy." In an interview with Angelus News, Dr. Papazian said that St. Gregory's writing style

> is reminiscent of St. Ephrem, the great fourth-century Syriac doctor. . . . His writing, even when it's not, strictly speaking, poetry, is always poetic. He loves to experiment. He invents words and constantly makes allusions to biblical passages.
>
> I sometimes think that he's what you'd get if you crossed Augustine and James Joyce. But his spirituality is also infused with the simple piety of the Desert Fathers; and, although he lived before him, there's an element of St. Francis in him, too. He's a synthesis of so many strands of Christian tradition.[18]

In February of 2021, Pope Francis gave St. Gregory an optional memorial on this day. St. Gregory's *Book of Lamentations* can be found online at www.stgregoryofnarek.am.

- Today offer some "heartfelt pleas of intercession." Ask St. Gregory to pray for you to always find "counsel toward virtue" (prayer 3).

Faith, that happy and favored word,
which lasts forever untarnished and unbounded,
honored together with charity and hope
brings the rewards of truly clear vision, perfect wisdom,
acquaintance with God and familiarity with the Exalted.
—St. Gregory of Narek[19]

March

ST. JOSEPH

M arch is the month of St. Joseph. In his Apostolic Letter *Patris Corde* [With a Father's Heart], Pope Francis called St. Joseph beloved, tender and loving, obedient, accepting, creatively courageous, a working father, and a father in the shadows.

> Each of us can discover in Joseph—the man who goes unnoticed, a daily, discreet, and hidden presence—an intercessor, a support and a guide in times of trouble. Saint Joseph reminds us that those who appear hidden or in the shadows can play an incomparable role in the history of salvation.[20]

What an inspiration St. Joseph is! Most of us live hidden lives with little fanfare, and yet our part in salvation history, like St. Joseph's, is incomparable. St. Joseph, pray for us.

Pray

Hail, Guardian of the Redeemer,
Spouse of the Blessed Virgin Mary.

To you God entrusted his only Son;
in you Mary placed her trust;
with you Christ became man.

Blessed Joseph, to us too,
show yourself a father
and guide us in the path of life.
Obtain for us grace, mercy, and courage,
and defend us from every evil. Amen.
— Prayer to St. Joseph, *Patris Corde*

Liturgical Color

Green in Ordinary Time
Purple in Lent

A Peek into March's Possibilities

(See Lent and Easter for more.)

MARCH 3
Optional Memorial of St. Katharine Drexel

MARCH 4
Optional Memorial of St. Casimir

MARCH 7
Memorial of Sts. Perpetua and Felicity

MARCH 8
Optional Memorial of St. John of God

MARCH 9
Optional Memorial of St. Frances of Rome

MARCH 17
Optional Memorial of St. Patrick

MARCH 19
Solemnity of St. Joseph

MARCH 25
Solemnity of the Annunciation of the Lord

March 3

ST. KATHARINE DREXEL
(1858–1955)

Religious, founder of the Sisters of the Blessed Sacrament;
patron of racial justice and philanthropists

Canonized on October 1, 2000, by Pope John Paul II, St. Katharine is only the second American-born saint to be recognized as such by the Church. Like her predecessor, Elizabeth Ann Seton, Katharine became an educator. She was born into a wealthy family and used the Drexel fortune to educate, evangelize, and spread the gospel.

Katharine's mother died when Katharine was a few weeks old, and her father later remarried. Katharine's father and devoted stepmother, Emma, were authentic Christians who genuinely lived their faith. They attended daily Mass with their children and opened their home to the needy three times a week, running a dispensary for those who needed free medicine. Emma earned the nickname "Lady Bountiful of Philadelphia" and was a role model to her daughters.

Katharine was always moved by the plight of indigenous people and people of color. Taking cues from her parents, she poured time, energy, and her own money into caring for the material needs of underprivileged and underrepresented groups, ignoring or standing up to those who harassed her and tried to thwart her efforts. As Fr. John Tolton wrote in a letter to her in 1891, which was quoted in the *Baltimore Sun* on the day of her canonization,

> It took the Catholic Church 100 years here in America to show forth such a person as yourself. . . . As I stand alone as the first Negro priest of America, so you, Katharine Drexel, stand alone as the first one to make such a sacrifice for the cause of a downtrodden race.[21]

Katharine founded Xavier University in New Orleans in 1915. It was the first (and only) Catholic university for African Americans in the United States. Her zeal and her mission of education spread. By the time she died, she could boast—though she never would—of more than five hundred nuns teaching in sixty-seven schools across the country.

Katharine died at the age of ninety-six, after many years of illness that had left her unable to work in an active capacity. Once she was confined to her bed, her work was prayer.

- St. Katharine lived the truth that nothing belongs to us and all that we have is from God. He's simply waiting for us to figure out how we'll use the gifts he's given us. What gifts has God given you that you want to use in service to him?

Let us open wide our hearts. It is joy which invites us. Press forward and fear nothing.

—St. Katherine Drexel[22]

March 4

ST. CASIMIR (1458–1484)

Patron of Poland and Lithuania

Born into royalty, Prince Casimir, son of King Casimir IV of Poland, reigned only briefly at the age of twenty-one, in his father's temporary absence. He was charming, pious, just, and also opposed to war. On one occasion, Casimir led his outnumbered, doomed-to-fail troops back home instead of leading them into battle, and his father punished him with a three-month confinement. Casimir was known after that as the "Peacemaker."

Casimir refused to marry and spent hours in prayer and penance, rejecting the comforts of his privileged life in order to strengthen his spiritual resolve. He died from lung disease at the age of twenty-six and was canonized in 1522, after a number of miracles were attributed to his intercession. Because of his tremendous devotion to Mary, the hymn *Omni die dic Maria* ("Daily, Daily, Sing to Mary") is often attributed to him, but it was possibly written by St. Bernard of Clairvaux.

- Casimir is a beautiful example of lifelong loyalty to God. Deep faith seems to come naturally to some people, and Casimir was one who received that gift.

  Do you feel that faith has come easily to you, or has it been hard-won? What can you do to deepen your loyalty to the Lord in spite of what others might think you should do with your life?

Daily, daily sing to Mary;
Sing, my soul, her praises due.
All her glorious actions cherish,
With the heart's devotion true. . . .

She is mighty to deliver;
Call her, trust her lovingly.
When the tempest rages round you,
She will calm the troubled sea.

—Hymn of St. Casimir[23]

March 7

STS. PERPETUA AND FELICITY
(DIED C. 203)

Martyred in Carthage, Africa;
patrons of mothers and expectant mothers

Perpetua and Felicity were young North African mothers who, along with fellow catechumens Revocatus, Secundulus, and Saturninus, were arrested, tried for their faith, then imprisoned and sentenced to face wild beasts in the arena. Their teacher, Saturus, was not arrested with them but surrendered to authorities in order to stay with the group.

Perpetua wrote in her diary that immediately after her Baptism, which occurred while the catechumens were under guard but before the nightmare of their imprisonment, "the Holy Ghost, on our coming out of the water, inspired me to pray for nothing but patience under corporal pains. A few days after this, we were put into prison."

Felicity was pregnant. Under Roman law, a pregnant woman could not be executed. Felicity gave birth just before her scheduled execution, and a fellow Christian adopted her child.

While in prison, Perpetua was devastated to be away from her six-month-old infant and begged to have him with her. Perpetua's mother was permitted to bring Perpetua's son to her, and she kept him with her until her death.

While in prison, Perpetua experienced a vision that confirmed her martyrdom:

I saw a golden ladder of marvelous height, reaching up even to heaven, and very narrow, so that persons could only ascend it one by one; and on the sides of the ladder was fixed every kind of iron weapon. There were there swords, lances, hooks, daggers; so that if any one went up carelessly, or not looking upwards, he would be torn to pieces and his flesh would cleave to the iron weapons. And under the ladder itself was crouching a dragon of wonderful size, who lay in wait for those who ascended, and frightened them from the ascent.

And Saturus went up first, who had subsequently delivered himself up freely on our account, not having been present at the time that we were taken prisoners. And he attained the top of the ladder, and turned towards me, and said to me, "Perpetua, I am waiting for you; but be careful that the dragon do not bite you." And I said, "In the name of the Lord Jesus Christ, he shall not hurt me." And from under the ladder itself, as if in fear of me, he slowly lifted up his head; and as I trod upon the first step, I trod upon his head.

And I went up, and I saw an immense extent of garden, and in the midst of the garden a white-haired man sitting in the dress of a shepherd, of a large stature, milking sheep; and standing around were many thousand white-robed ones. And he raised his head, and looked upon me, and said to me, "You are welcome, daughter." And he called me, and from the cheese as he was milking he gave me as it were a little cake, and I received it with folded hands; and I ate it, and all who stood around said Amen.

And at the sound of their voices I was awakened, still tasting a sweetness which I cannot describe. And I immediately related this to my brother, and we understood that it was to be a passion, and we ceased henceforth to have any hope in this world.[24]

The full text of *The Passion of Saints Perpetua and Felicity* is available at various sites online.

- Perpetua's diary is a powerful and inspiring witness to our faith. When we read such raw and powerful stories, we should pray that when we meet Jesus, we too will hear, "You are welcome, daughter."

Do we have the courage to openly proclaim the name of Jesus wherever we are? Let's pray that we always will and that one day we will taste that "sweetness which we cannot describe."

"Father," said I, "do you see, let us say, this vessel lying here to be a little pitcher, or something else?" And he said, "I see it to be so."

And I replied to him, "Can it be called by any other name than what it is?" And he said, "No."

"Neither can I call myself anything else than what I am, a Christian."

—Perpetua speaking to her father at her trial when he begged her to renounce her faith[25]

March 8

ST. JOHN OF GOD (1495–1550)

Soldier, healthcare worker, servant to the poor and sick; patron of hospital workers, nurses, booksellers

John was kidnapped from his home in Portugal when he was eight years old. He became homeless, and at various times he was a shepherd, a soldier, a worker on behalf of captive Christians in Africa, and, after his conversion, a bookseller.

While he was selling books and religious articles from town to town, John heard a sermon by St. John of Ávila that so moved him that he began performing public acts of outrageous penance, such as tearing his hair and running wildly through the streets. Considered demented, he was confined to an asylum, where he was beaten and frequently endured solitary confinement.

St. John of Ávila visited John, advising him to channel his zealous faith into service to others rather than against himself. John vowed to do so, and he gave the rest of his life to serving the sick and poor, intent on helping them avoid the treatment he had received. His work eventually led to the founding of the Brothers Hospitallers, a religious order serving the sick and needy.

- Some say John of God was overly zealous, some say he went berserk for a time, while others insist he was a fervent convert. Perhaps all of these words describe the various stages of conversion.

  Have you gone through a period in your faith life that you questioned or regretted? How did you emerge from that time with a healthier grasp of your faith?

When you feel depressed, have recourse to the Passion of Jesus Christ, our Lord, and his precious wounds, and you will feel great consolation.

—St. John of God[26]

March 9

ST. FRANCES OF ROME
(1384–1440)

Wife, mother, religious, mystic; patron of drivers and motorists, Benedictine oblates

Why is a fifteenth-century mystic the patron saint of motorists? Pope Pius XI so named Frances in 1925. Legend says that a lantern-bearing angel lit the road before her to protect her whenever she traveled. It is fitting: Frances too blazed light wherever she went.

Frances was the kind of rebel and friend we can all admire. She followed the promptings of God over the conventions of her time yet retained a clear sense of ultimate obedience to the Lord. Though she was drawn to religious life, her parents selected a husband for her, and she conceded. When her mother-in-law died, sixteen-year-old Frances was put in charge of managing the entire extended family and their estate. She was truly a working wife and mother, sustained by visions, ecstasies, and closeness to the Lord. She would remain happily married to Lorenzo Ponziano for many years.

When Frances discovered that her sister-in-law Vannozza (the wife of her husband's brother) also harbored a heart for service, the women set out to serve the poor, despite the loud protests of their wealthy in-laws. Their husbands revered them and refused to interfere with their charitable work. They also supported their inclination for prayer when their daily work was done.

During a famine in Rome, Frances overruled her father-in-law and ordered that no one who needed food would be turned away from the family's doors. More than once she turned the family home into a hospital. She personally collected firewood and medicine, and she even begged for alms to help the poor. Her infectious faith and unyielding spirit attracted a group of women who wanted to live lives of service. Loosely organized as oblates in the Benedictine tradition, the women carried on Frances' service to the poor and sick.

When Lorenzo died in 1436, Frances became the oblates' superior, and she lived the final four years of her life with them. She finally achieved her girlhood dream of religious life.

- Do you ever question your vocation? Have you put dreams of some kind on hold? Today ask God to continue guiding your life, step-by-step, and trust that he will use all your talents at various stages, even unpredictably.

Are you crying because you want to do God's will or because you want God to do your will?

— St. Frances of Rome's confessor[27]

March 17

ST. PATRICK (C. 385–461)

Bishop; patron of engineers and Ireland

There are only a few historical facts available about St. Patrick, but his *Confession,* which can be found in its entirety online, contains helpful and genuine details. He was probably born in England or Scotland, and as a teen, he was kidnapped and sold into slavery in Ireland. He prayed constantly during his captivity—"I used to get up for prayer before daylight, through snow, through frost, through rain, and I felt no harm"—and his faith grew by leaps and bounds.[28] He later wrote, "The love of God and his fear increased in me more and more, and the faith grew in me, and the spirit was roused, so that, in a single day, I have said as many as a hundred prayers."[29]

Patrick escaped from slavery and studied for the priesthood. He returned to Ireland as a missionary bishop, after a dream in which he heard the Irish calling him back. He wrote,

[I]n a vision of the night, I saw a man whose name was Victoricus coming as if from Ireland with innumerable letters, and he gave me one of them, and I read the beginning of the letter: "The Voice of the Irish"; and as I was reading the beginning of the letter I seemed at that moment to hear the voice of those who were beside the forest of Foclut which is near the western sea, and they were crying as if with one voice: "We beg you, holy youth, that you shall come and shall walk again among us." And I was stung intensely in my heart so that I could read no more, and thus I awoke.[30]

Humble—and also embarrassed by his lack of education—Patrick nevertheless persevered in sharing God's word.

- "St. Patrick's Breastplate" is a well-known prayer of complete devotion to the Lord. You can find gorgeous and edifying vocal and instrumental versions of this prayer online. Search for "The Deer's Cry" and "Lorica of St. Patrick," as well as "St. Patrick's Breastplate." Pray for Christ to be everything to you, as he was to St. Patrick.

Christ with me,
Christ before me,
Christ behind me,
Christ in me,
Christ beneath me,
Christ above me,
Christ on my right,
Christ on my left,
Christ when I lie down,
Christ when I sit down,
Christ when I arise,
Christ in the heart of every man who thinks of me,

Christ in the mouth of everyone who speaks of me,
Christ in every eye that sees me,
Christ in every ear that hears me.
                    —Excerpt from St. Patrick's Breastplate[31]

March 19

SOLEMNITY OF ST. JOSEPH

*Patron of the Universal Church, carpenters, fathers,
expectant mothers, laborers, social justice, travelers,
immigrants, house hunters, the dying, a happy death;
patron against doubt*

Connect

How easy it is to overlook this steadfast saint! We take him for granted because he's always there, next to Jesus and Mary, ready to teach, guard, protect, and shepherd. And yet his life, like Mary's, had been turned upside down.

Imagine you're a typical turn-of-the-millennium man, engaged to a lovely woman, planning your future together, when suddenly she tells you she's pregnant. The child is clearly not yours. What do you do?

Joseph, the just man, tried to obey God's law by breaking the engagement. In his kindness and compassion, he planned to do so quietly, so as not to bring shame and attention to Mary. Only when God spoke to him in a dream did he realize that God's plan was that he proceed with the marriage. In humility and love for the Lord, Joseph moved forward. What trust he displayed!

There have been times when I thought I was being faithful and obedient, only to discover that I'd been interpreting God's ways rigidly and that God actually expected the *unexpected* of me. St. Joseph, pray for us to genuinely discern God's will.

To Ponder or Do

The challenge on this solemnity is not dreaming up ways to honor this great saint but narrowing things down to one or two. Here are a few ideas:

- Go to Mass and thank God for Joseph's example.

- Pray to St. Joseph, entrusting the impossible to him. I prayed to him daily for my husband's conversion after my own conversion to Catholicism. I was convinced my husband would *never* convert—he made it clear that he wouldn't. Five years after entrusting this impossible request to St. Joseph, my husband was received into the Church.

- The St. Joseph table is a Sicilian tradition. Overload your table with a grand Italian feast that includes special breads and cream puffs. Have fragrant flowers to add to the festive feel.

No time to cook? St. Joseph doesn't mind. Buy takeout and grab treats from the bakery. Celebrations don't have to be homemade to have meaning.

And remember, even though St. Joseph's day falls in Lent, it's always a solemnity, which outranks our Lenten observance. Mother Church wants us to have a party. St. Joseph is worth it.

- Read Pope Leo XIII's short and accessible encyclical on devotion to St. Joseph, *Quamquam pluries*, August 15, 1889, which can be found at the Vatican website vatican.va.

- Have you ever felt that the Lord was speaking to you through a dream? How did you discern whether your dream had genuine spiritual significance or was just a flight of fancy?

Pray

Dear Lord, St. Joseph seemed content to play a humble role in the life of Jesus and Mary, but what sacrifices he must have made and felt! He was a husband and father but not in traditional ways, and his role required that he give up a normal life. He must have had to let go of many dreams and expectations. Help me look to St. Joseph this month as I deal with dreams, expectations, and the things in my life that are holy but difficult surprises. Give me the faith of St. Joseph and his willingness to serve you.

March 25

SOLEMNITY OF THE ANNUNCIATION OF THE LORD

Connect

How do we connect with Mary—the Immaculate Conception, the mother of Jesus, queen of heaven and earth? She was conceived without sin, said yes to God when he asked the incomprehensible of her, and stands at the right hand of God in heaven. Those are enormous shoes to step into.

And yet God made each and every one of us to try on such shoes and make them fit. We are all called to say yes to God when he asks the incomprehensible of us. What that is looks different in each of our lives, but we know it when we see, hear, or feel it, don't we?

God allows us to face uncertainties day after day: the choice that's hard to make, the self-sacrifice required in relationships, the charity needed to interact with challenging people, the call to forgive those who have hurt us deeply, the discipline to live out our faith. Every day we are presented with choices.

When Gabriel appeared to Mary and announced that she was to conceive and bear Jesus, he said, "Do not be afraid" (Luke 1:30). Mary, who could have said no to God's request, said instead, "Behold, I am the handmaid of the Lord. May it be done to me according to your word" (1:38). When God comes before us—in the form of choices, sacrifices, relationships, demands for charity, calls to forgiveness, and invitations to faithful living—we too have the option to say yes or no.

- What inexplicable thing is God asking of you today? Do the shoes look too big, or are you eager to step into them? Wherever you are, ask God to help you surrender to his will as fully and completely as Mary did.

To Ponder or Do

- Read Luke 1:26-38; consider the possible ways God is asking you to surrender to his word.

- Consider Mary as a model of the Church at prayer. In his general audience on September 10, 1997, Pope John Paul II said,

In all probability Mary was absorbed in prayer when the angel Gabriel came to her house in Nazareth and greeted her. This prayerful setting certainly supported the Blessed Virgin in her reply to the angel and in her generous assent to the mystery of the Incarnation.

In the Annunciation scene, artists have almost always depicted Mary in a prayerful attitude.[32]

- Look up various paintings of the Annunciation, and use them in your prayer time to deepen your appreciation for Mary and the choice she faced. There are many beautiful imaginings of this moment, from Leonardo da Vinci to Fra Angelico to Henry Ossawa Tanner.

- Feast! Even though the Annunciation invariably falls on a day in Lent, a solemnity overrides Lenten observances. As with St. Joseph's day, this is a day to celebrate. Consider making or buying angel food cake or your favorite indulgence for dessert tonight. Did you give up a food you love for Lent? You can have it today. Some European traditions encourage waffles for feast days, especially the Annunciation. Waffles and whipped cream for dinner, anyone?

Pray

Lord, I often feel far from "handmaid of the Lord" status. It's not always easy for me to say yes to everything you ask of me, and the questions aren't always as clear as this one was to Mary.

Since I don't experience angels appearing and voicing your requests, please help me discern the best I can: which demands on my life come from you? Which ones come from the world or my own head? Help me to hear your voice, Lord, and to say yes to *you* as sincerely and lovingly as Mary did.

Lent and Easter

THE PASSION, DEATH, AND RESURRECTION OF OUR LORD

When my youngest daughter was six years old, her big sisters asked her what she was going to give up for Lent. When she replied that she didn't know yet, one of them suggested she give up being sassy to her sisters. In full-on defiance mode, my youngest wheeled on her accusers and cried out, "No! I'm going to give up something *meaningful*!"

We didn't actually require our six-year-old to give up *anything* during Lent, of course. Our girls were raised with the liturgical seasons though, so Lent was a pretty big deal at our house. It would have been hard for even a six-year-old to ignore that *something* out of the ordinary was happening.

We tailored our observances to the ages and stages of the girls over the years. We let them choose small sacrifices on their own when they were younger, and they grew into what the Church asked of them as they matured. The key was always the word that my youngest had somehow picked up on: meaningful.

Lent is a time of preparation for Easter, a time to prepare our hearts and minds for the joy and mystery of the resurrection. The Church offers us a foundation for that preparation:

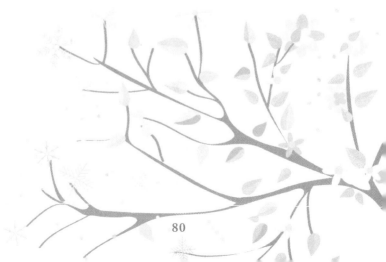

prayer, fasting, and almsgiving. What do those things look like in our homes?

Here the Church offers us generous leeway. We are free to tailor, tinker, and figure out what works best for us as we strive to grow closer to God through the gift of this penitential season.

The Lenten obligations for adults are fasting (ages eighteen to fifty-nine) and abstinence from meat (ages fourteen and up) on Ash Wednesday and Good Friday and abstinence from meat on all Fridays in Lent. (Pregnant and nursing women are exempt, of course, as are those with health concerns or conditions.) We're encouraged to consider keeping our Good Friday fast until Holy Saturday night, if possible, as a way to honor our Lord.[33]

Obligations for prayer and almsgiving are not spelled out definitively, so be creative and figure out what works well for you and your family. The point again is to make the season personally meaningful. Are your prayers, your charitable giving, and your fasting and abstinence drawing you closer to the Lord? If so, welcome to a meaningful Lent.

Pray

Lord, as I enter into Lent and prepare my heart for the joy of Easter, help me dig deep. Lead me to the practices and prayers that will draw me closer to you. As I observe this season prayerfully, help me find a more meaningful relationship with you.

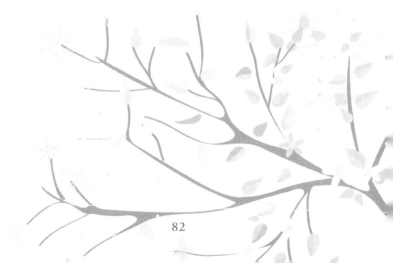

Liturgical Color

Purple in Lent
White during Easter
Red for Pentecost

A Peek into Lent and Easter's Possibilities

(Be sure to see February, March, and April for specific feast days and saints to celebrate throughout the season. The Solemnity of St. Joseph—March 19—and the Solemnity of the Annunciation—March 25—usually fall during Lent.)

ASH WEDNESDAY

OBSERVING LENT
Ideas for Making Prayer, Fasting, and Almsgiving More Meaningful

HOLY WEEK
Palm Sunday of the Lord's Passion
The Paschal Triduum: Holy Thursday, Good Friday, Holy Saturday, and Easter

OCTAVE OF EASTER

DIVINE MERCY SUNDAY

SOLEMNITY OF THE ASCENSION

SOLEMNITY OF PENTECOST

Ash Wednesday

Connect

Some years we head into Lent knowing—or presuming to know—exactly what God is calling us to do. Other years we're scrambling on Ash Wednesday, wondering what we can do to draw closer to God and serve others during this season. When it comes to penitential practices, do we give up coffee, complaining, snacking, wine, TV, or internet distractions? Sometimes the corporal sacrifice comes easily, but the deepening of prayer seems elusive and challenging.

Lent always involves the three disciplines of prayer, almsgiving, and penance, and we practice these as a means of growing in our love for the Lord and for one another, especially those most in need. As Pope Francis said in his Lenten Message for 2018,

Lent summons us, and enables us, to come back to the Lord wholeheartedly and in every aspect of our life. . . .

. . . The Church . . . offers us in the Lenten season the soothing remedy of prayer, almsgiving and fasting.

By devoting more time to *prayer*, we enable our hearts to root out our secret lies and forms of self-deception, and then to find the consolation God offers. He is our Father and he wants us to live life well.

Almsgiving sets us free from greed and helps us to regard our neighbor as a brother or sister. What I possess is never mine alone. How I would like almsgiving to become a genuine style of life for each of us! How I would like us, as Christians, to follow the example of the Apostles and see in the sharing of our possessions a tangible witness of the communion that is ours in the Church! . . .

Fasting weakens our tendency to violence; it disarms us and becomes an important opportunity for growth. On the one hand, it allows us to experience what the destitute and the starving have to endure. On the other hand, it expresses our own spiritual hunger and thirst for life in God. Fasting wakes us up. It makes us more attentive to God and our neighbor. It revives our desire to obey God, who alone is capable of satisfying our hunger.[34]

Ultimately, perhaps the most important Lenten sacrifice is simply acknowledging that we're not the ones in control. The most meaningful Lent is the one that is filled with God's work, not ours.

To Ponder or Do

- Go to Mass if you can. Ash Wednesday is not a holy day of obligation, but it's a beautiful way to begin Lent. If you can't get to Mass, look up the readings for the day. Focus on the intimacy of God calling you to return to him with your whole heart.

- There's no rule about what to do with the ashes you receive. Some people wear them all day, while others wash them off. Either choice can be an act of love. Some opt to leave them on as a beautiful way to show the world that they love the Lord and their faith. On the other hand, some spend their day with people who are antagonistic or hostile to the faith; those hearts might be further hardened when faced with a display they don't understand. Decide what's right for you and your circumstances.

- Consider these words from Pope Benedict XVI's Message for Lent 2013:

  The Christian life consists in continuously scaling the mountain to meet God and then coming back down, bearing the love and strength drawn from him, so as to serve our brothers and sisters with God's own love. . . .

  Dear brothers and sisters, in this season of Lent, as we prepare to celebrate the event of the Cross and Resurrection—in which the love of God redeemed the world and shone its light upon history—I express my wish that all of you may spend this precious time rekindling your faith in Jesus Christ, so as to enter with him into the dynamic of love for the Father and for every brother and sister that we encounter in our lives.[35]

- Are you still unsure of what you want to do this Lent? It's okay; you're not being graded. Every day of Lent is a new beginning. Ask God to open a door to growth that you hadn't thought of or considered. And with St.

Augustine pray, "Stir us up, and call us back; inflame us, and draw us to Thee; stir us up, and grow sweet unto us; let us now love Thee, let us run after Thee."[36]

Pray

Lord, in Scripture you tell us that you are "slow to anger and rich in mercy" (Nehemiah 9:17). Pour your kindness upon me today and throughout this Lenten season, as you show me new and surprising ways to grow closer to you. Soften my heart to your word and to your ways.

Observing Lent

IDEAS FOR MAKING PRAYER, FASTING, AND ALMSGIVING MORE MEANINGFUL

Prayer

Increase your prayer time. Do you have a time set aside for personal prayer? If you do, consider increasing the amount of time or perhaps adding a new devotion. If you don't have a formalized time, take a look at your day, and see if you can schedule ten minutes with God. Don't be hard on yourself, though, when life interrupts you and your prayer life seems imperfect.

Pray a daily offering. This is a way to give your whole day to God in one fell swoop. It can be a formal morning offering, such as this traditional prayer:

> O Jesus, through the Immaculate Heart of Mary, I offer you my prayers, works, joys, and sufferings of this day, in union with the Holy Sacrifice of the Mass throughout the world. I offer them for all the intentions of your Sacred Heart: the salvation of souls, reparation for sin, the reunion of all Christians. I offer them for the intentions of our bishops and all apostles of prayer, and especially and in particular for those recommended by the Holy Father this month. Amen.

Or you can pray such an offering in your own words, such as "Dear Lord, I give you this day: all that I think, all that I say, all that I do, I give to you."

Choose a prayer spot. Pick a place you can make your own. Within family life, that sometimes seems impossible, but even your bed—with a Bible or your favorite prayer book on the nightstand and the door closed—can become your sacred space at home.

Pray in new places. Chat with Jesus or pray formal prayers on the way to work, while walking the dog, or while working out. Pray in the shower, every time you're in the grocery store, or while you're mowing the lawn. Talk to God as you're throwing dinner together, when you're in line for school drop-off and pick-up, while you do morning or evening chores or a nighttime routine. Is there a place in your life where God feels far away—work? school?—or where you feel alone? Say a prayer every time you're in that place.

Pray with someone else. If you're married and have never set aside a regular time to pray with your spouse, consider doing so. Do you have a faithful friend you see regularly but never pray with? Ask her if she'd like to start.

Weekday Mass. If you can make it work, try getting to Mass more often. Is there a day of the week you can slip it in? The peace and quiet of a weekday Mass along with the power of the Eucharist can offer a recharge when you think you have nothing more to give.

Adoration of the Blessed Sacrament. While some can manage a regular weekly hour at their parish, others might duck into church for a few minutes with the Lord. You don't have to have a holy *hour;* it can be a holy five or ten minutes.

A new or renewed devotion. The Rosary, or just a morning decade. The Chaplet of Divine Mercy. The Litany of Humility. The day's Mass readings. *Lectio divina* ("divine reading," praying with Scripture). A saint-a-day book. Spontaneous, conversational prayer. A daily devotional book or magazine.

Stations of the Cross and Bible study. Attend Stations on Friday nights in Lent, or pray the stations at home, on your own or with family or friends. Perhaps there's a new Scripture or Lenten book study starting up at your parish that you could join.

Read a book you've been meaning to read. Who's your favorite Catholic writer? Is there a spiritual classic you've been meaning to get to? Spending time with spiritual masters is its own kind of prayer time.

Journal. Start or return to a gratitude journal. Take a few minutes every day to tell the Lord that you noticed a gift he gave you. Or keep a journal of your favorite prayers; take some quiet time to copy them into your notebook. Consider keeping a journal of Lenten insights: What are you noticing this year? What's easy; what's hard? Is the season proceeding as you thought it would?

Visual reminders: I have a crown of thorns that a dear friend gave me when I was received into the Church. It sits on the mantle every Lent and acts as a silent prompt for prayers of thanksgiving and humility. What symbols or decorations work for you?

Offer it up. Practice the habit of offering your suffering as a prayer. Every time you have to tackle your most dreaded chore at home or a tough task at work, offer it up for a specific intention. When you are bored, offer up your boredom. If you have serious physical pain or are dealing with an illness, ask God to transform your suffering for the good of another soul.

Examination of conscience. Do a brief examen every day. You can consult the Spiritual Exercises of St. Ignatius Loyola for this. He taught a daily examen that consists of a few simple steps: (1) place yourself in God's presence, and ask him to enlighten you through the next steps; (2) give thanks for specifics of the day; (3) review your day with honesty; (4) ask for forgiveness, help, or healing where needed; (5) ask the Lord to help you grow in concrete ways the following day.

If this interests you, do a deeper dive and learn more about St. Ignatius.

Go to Confession. Dorothy Parker, a twentieth-century American writer, once said of her trade, "Hate to write, love having written." That line characterizes how most of us feel about getting ourselves to Confession: "Hate to go, love having gone." There's no better time to get there. You'll love the fact you did.

Keep it meaningful. Don't try to do it all. Pick one or two things. Let your Lent be filled with God's work in you, through you, and for you.

Fasting

Decide what's meaningful to *you*. Fasting is meant to help us grow in discipline, self-control, and reliance on God. As Lent begins, there are lots of conversations among friends and on the internet about what constitutes a meaningful sacrifice. Some will scoff at giving up "trivialities" such as coffee or sugar, but for someone who's attached, forgoing these daily addictions is no small feat.

Tune out the noise, and tune in to what God is telling *you*. Ask him to reveal what you're really attached to, then ask him to help you give it up for forty days for his sake. His whisper is sometimes louder than we'd like to admit, and it's certainly more important than other people's noise.

Don't worry about whether you're giving up something "good" or something "bad." A sacrifice is defined as giving up an objective good for a greater good—in this case, growing closer to God. Some people argue that giving up a bad habit, such as complaining, isn't a true sacrifice in the context of Lent. I don't want to argue with the arguers, but let's face it: if it's hard to give up, then we're inordinately attached to it, and letting go of it *is* a sacrifice.

The main difference here is simply what happens at Easter: if we give up an objective good, we get to reclaim it on Easter. If we let go of a bad habit, we're permanently better off. Whatever I choose to give up, it's between God and me. There are many paths to meaningful sacrifice.

Make a list. Write down all your ideas for sacrificial fasting. Make an extensive list. Then remind yourself that you're not Wonder Woman and that Lent isn't about conquering the world. It's about growing a little closer to God today, this week, this Lent. Pick one thing, maybe two. Being realistic is a legitimate path to holiness.

Think outside the box. Perhaps you want to choose a Lenten challenge you've never tackled before. Remember, what really matters is that this sacrifice makes sense for *you*. Some of the following ideas may seem trivial; some might sound huge. Some may be new to you, while others are old-school. We're all in different places on the attachment path. *You* get to figure out what will work best for you.

Try giving up one of the following:

Music in the car, at home, on your commute
Netflix, streaming, bingeing
Background noise (TV, radio, music, sports)
Complaining
Gossip
Worrying: turn every worry into a new chant: "I have radical trust in Jesus."
Pessimism
Red meat or all meat
Seafood
Alcohol
Snacks
Dessert or sugar or cheese
Fast food or takeout
Lattes
A food you adore (Who cares if no one else thinks that giving up hummus is a sacrifice?)
Carbonated beverages
Bread
Caffeine

Wearing jewelry or other accessories
Makeup
Social media
Mindless phone scrolling
Unnecessary spending
Time (Adding prayer or volunteer time means sacrificing time somewhere else.)

Having trouble making a decision? Consider giving up something different each day or each week of Lent.

Almsgiving

Up your tithe at church. Increase your weekly or monthly giving. Simple!

Choose a charity to be the recipient of your sacrificial fasting. Did you give up something that's now saving you money? No takeout or lattes, meatless meals? I don't usually advocate scrupulosity, but let's get scrupulous with the math. Figure out how much money you're saving, and funnel it into your Lenten charitable giving.

In addition, most of us have a coin jar or bowl for spare quarters and dimes. Keep the jar in a prominent place during Lent. Involve the family, and choose a charity to donate the coins to after Easter.

Give in to that mailing or online plea for help. You get their mailings all the time, it's a cause you support, yet you never get around to sending them money. Or perhaps you use a website or service that runs on donations, and you've never donated? Do it now.

Get rid of extra stuff. You've been meaning to declutter, right? It doesn't have to be a huge project. Just organize this room, clear out that closet, and donate what you don't truly need—as long as the items are in excellent shape. Simplify and consolidate your wardrobe.

On the fence about an object or a piece of clothing? Donate.

Give your time. Give yourself. Spend time with someone who needs your company. Write letters. (Remember those?) Visit a lonely relative or acquaintance. Slow down, and spend intentional time with family and friends. Have a date night, and let your spouse run the agenda. Play a game—the one you usually say no to—with your kids. Give up the frantic pace of life, and give others the treasure of your genuine presence.

Holy Week

PALM SUNDAY
OF THE LORD'S PASSION

Every year the Palm Sunday liturgy is the same, and every year it's immensely moving. Every year we stand accused as part of the assembly, the sea of voices, the crowd that is calling for the crucifixion of Jesus.

In his 2021 Palm Sunday homily, Pope Francis put it beautifully:

From the start, Jesus leaves us amazed. His people give him a solemn welcome, yet he enters Jerusalem on a lowly colt. His people expect a powerful liberator at Passover, yet he comes to bring the Passover to fulfilment by sacrificing himself. His people are hoping to triumph over the Romans by the sword, but Jesus comes to celebrate God's triumph through the cross.

What happened to those people who in a few days' time went from shouting "Hosanna" to crying out "Crucify him"? . . . They were following an *idea* of the Messiah rather than *the* Messiah. They *admired* Jesus, but they did not let themselves be *amazed* by him.

Amazement is not the same as admiration. Admiration can be worldly, since it follows its own tastes and expectations. Amazement . . . remains open to others and to the newness they bring. . . . To admire Jesus is not enough. We have to follow in his footsteps, to let ourselves be challenged by him; to pass from admiration to amazement.[37]

To Ponder or Do

- When you receive a palm at Mass this year, ask yourself, "Do I admire Jesus in the worldly manner Pope Francis describes, or rather, as the pope says, am I amazed by him, letting him challenge me?" When was the last time Jesus amazed you?

- Do you ever feel that you are following an idea of Jesus rather than following Jesus himself? Jesus wants a genuine relationship with you. Ask Jesus to bowl you over this Holy Week.

- Spend some time with the following words from Church Father St. Andrew of Crete, and consider what it means to "be the garment" that is spread before Jesus.

Let us run to accompany him as he hastens toward his passion, and imitate those who met him then, not by covering his path with garments, olive branches or palms, but by doing all we can to prostrate ourselves before him by being humble and by trying to live as he would wish. Then we shall be able to receive the Word at his coming, and God, whom no limits can contain, will be within us. . . .

We who have been baptized into Christ must ourselves be the garments that we spread before him. Now that the crimson stains of our sins have been washed away in the saving waters of baptism and we have become white as pure wool, let us present the conqueror of death, not with mere branches of palms but with the real rewards of his victory.

Let our souls take the place of the welcoming branches as we join today in the children's holy song: *Blessed is he who comes in the name of the Lord. Blessed is the king of Israel.*[38]

- In what ways has Jesus challenged you this Lent? What newness or blessing has he brought to your life?

Pray

Lord, as I enter into Holy Week, inspire me so that I never follow a mere *idea* of you, allowing myself to simply go through the motions. Let me feel genuine, holy amazement at what you did for me through your passion, death, and resurrection. Make me aware of what you are doing for me *right now*, during *this* Holy Week.

THE PASCHAL TRIDUUM:

HOLY THURSDAY, GOOD FRIDAY, HOLY SATURDAY, AND EASTER

Connect

Lent comes to a quiet close on the afternoon of Holy Thursday, and we now climb to the summit of the liturgical year, the Triduum, which means "three days." This is the period from Holy Thursday evening until Easter Sunday evening. The Church considers these three days as one liturgy spread over three services: the Mass of the Lord's Supper (Holy Thursday), Good Friday of the Lord's passion, and the Mass of the Resurrection of the Lord (Easter).

Having come into the Catholic Church at an Easter Vigil brimming with pageantry and joy, I have immense affection for this spectacular Mass, as well as for the services leading up to this holiest of nights. But not every year before or since has been perfect or memorable. Sometimes I attended the Triduum alone and felt quite lonely. One year, before my husband's conversion, I stayed home on Holy Thursday and Good Friday because I sensed that this was what my family needed in spite of my personal yearning to be in church.

The Lord understands family life. Making it to every Holy Week liturgy isn't a litmus test of a family's faithfulness. The Triduum is a banquet to which we're invited, and every time we're able to say yes to the invitation, God seems to offer us something new. But he doesn't punish us when we can't show up. Easter morning Mass fulfills the Sunday obligation every bit as much as the Easter Vigil does, and Holy Thursday and Good Friday, as gorgeous as they are, are not holy days of obligation. As always, talk to God about your schedule and your life, and follow his lead.

To Ponder or Do

- If you've never attended the Easter Vigil, consider giving it a try. Yes, it's long, but it's also the summit of the liturgical year, full of drama, pageantry, pomp, and glory. There are catechumens wearing identifying garments—sometimes robes, sometimes simple baptismal stoles around their necks. There are Baptisms, triumphant transformations. The Easter Vigil is the spectacular culmination of Holy Week.

- If you can't attend the Easter Vigil Mass, participate in as much of the Triduum as you can. If you have very young children or a conflicting work schedule, this can be a challenge. Just do what works for you. Don't be harder on yourself than the Church is.

- If you are able to participate in the entirety of the Triduum, thank God for the privilege and for the spiritual nourishment he's providing for you on the journey toward the joy of Easter.

- On Good Friday, you can start praying the Divine Mercy Novena, which is prayed from Good Friday through Divine Mercy Sunday, the Sunday after Easter. (You can find the Novena of Divine Mercy at www.thedivinemercy.org/message/devotions/novena.)

- Try to slow down this week. That's easier said than done! With Easter Sunday and perhaps family gatherings approaching, it's natural to get caught up in the details of meal planning, visitor logistics, and schedules. Take a few minutes each day of Holy Week to just breathe and be with God.

- Be solemn but not too solemn. Perhaps you're the only Catholic in your extended family, or you have young children. The local Easter egg hunt with your child's best friend might not fall at the most convenient or desirable time during Holy Week, but be flexible with kids. Wouldn't it be lovely if everyone celebrated the great fifty days of Easter and moved all the parties to that period? But that's not the case in our diverse society, and God gets that. Be in the world but not of it, and focus on radiating Christ's love to those around you.

- Whether you attend the Vigil or Easter Sunday Mass, the party is just starting. Plan to keep the Easter decorations up for at least the first week (the Octave of Easter) or possibly for the full fifty days of the Easter season.

Pray

Lord, in giving us the gift of the liturgical year, you have bestowed immense riches on us. Through Holy Week and the Triduum, you lead us to the peak of the liturgical mountain. Thank you for your expansive kindness and loving attention to our humble human needs: our desire for signs and symbols, for sensory experiences. You feed and nourish our bodies and souls.

Thank you, Lord Jesus, for the gift of the Church and her liturgical year.

OCTAVE OF EASTER

Why do we call it an octave? "Octave," for "eight," indicates a period of eight days in the Church year during which we celebrate a feast so enormous that its joy cannot be corralled into a single feast day.

The Octave of Easter runs from Easter Sunday until the following Sunday. Each day is the highest of feasts—a solemnity—and each day is worth celebrating. For example, even though every Friday of the year is meant to be penitential in nature, with a sacrifice of our choosing to be offered during Ordinary Time, the Friday after Easter is *not* a penitential day. Feast to your heart's content for eight straight days.

Contemplate these words:

> Let us establish a permanent Spring season in our heart through "yes" often repeated to all of God's permissions and wills.
>
> —St. Francisca Salesia Aviat[39]

DIVINE MERCY SUNDAY

The Easter party's been in full swing for a week, and we've reached the conclusion of the Octave of Easter: Divine Mercy Sunday. Pope John Paul II established this feast for the worldwide Church on April 30, 2000, the day that St. Faustina was canonized. It was a great joy for him to declare "this humble daughter of Poland" a saint.

See if your parish is praying the Chaplet of Divine Mercy at 3:00 p.m. on this feast day, or pray the chaplet at home or with friends. As Pope John Paul II, in his homily for the canonization of Sr. Maria Faustina Kowalska on April 30, 2000, said, "The message of divine mercy is also implicitly *a message about the value of every human being.* Each person is precious in God's eyes; Christ gave his life for each one; to everyone the Father gives his Spirit and offers intimacy."[40]

"For the sake of his sorrowful passion, have mercy on us and on the whole world."

SOLEMNITY OF THE ASCENSION

"But you will receive power when the holy Spirit comes upon you, and you will be my witnesses in Jerusalem, throughout Judea and Samaria, and to the ends of the earth." When he had said this, as they were looking on, he was lifted up, and a cloud took him from their sight. (Acts 1:8-9)

Forty days after Easter, we celebrate Ascension Thursday, though in some dioceses, the liturgy for this feast is moved to the seventh Sunday after Easter.

Have you ever wondered how the disciples reacted to the ascension of Jesus? What must they have thought at this unexpected turn of events? After giving their lives up to and for him, they'd lost Jesus to the misery of his crucifixion and death. Then they rejoiced at his resurrection and spent the next forty days continuing to learn from him. They must have cheered and celebrated, thinking, "Huzzah, he's back!" And now he was leaving them? *Again?*

We can only imagine their confusion. Jesus gave them a clue about what was to come: "But you will receive power when the holy Spirit comes upon you" (Acts 1:8).

The apostles didn't yet know about what was to come at Pentecost, but Jesus did. He knew that further strength and empowerment were on the way. Although his disciples didn't yet understand what was in store for their future, they trusted him. They believed him when he said, "And behold, I am with you always, until the end of the age" (Matthew 28:20).

- Have you ever been confused by what God has allowed to happen to you? When everything seems to be unfolding in ways you don't want and didn't expect, is your reaction protest and confusion or trust?

SOLEMNITY OF PENTECOST

Ten days after Ascension Thursday and fifty days after Easter, we observe Pentecost Sunday. "Pentecost" comes from the Greek word for "fiftieth." The people of Israel celebrated Pentecost as the fiftieth day after their departure from Egypt and the day on which God gave the Ten Commandments to Moses. So it was that many Jews were gathered in Jerusalem when the Holy Spirit descended upon the disciples of Jesus (see Exodus 34; Acts 2).

Pentecost is also known as the origin or birthday of the Church. It was the moment at which the followers of Jesus were filled with the Holy Spirit and were empowered to "make disciples of all nations, baptizing them in the name of the Father, and of the Son, and of the holy Spirit, teaching them to observe all that I have commanded you" (Matthew 28:19-20).

As the *Catechism of the Catholic Church* points out (see 732), Pentecost was the event through which the Holy Trinity was fully revealed. The disciples had met and knew God the Father and Jesus the Son, and now—with the gift of the Holy Spirit—the reality of the Holy Trinity was made manifest.

In his 2021 Pentecost homily, Pope Francis said,

> "The Paraclete will come, whom I will send from the Father" (Jn 15:26). With these words, Jesus promises the disciples the Holy Spirit, the definitive gift, the gift of gifts. He speaks of it using a particular, mysterious expression: *Paraclete*. Today we welcome this word, which is not easy to translate as it contains several meanings. Paraclete, in essence, means two things: *Comforter* and *Advocate*.[41]

Comforter. Advocate. The Lord has given us everything we need to carry on his work. In Matthew 28:16-20, we encounter "The Great Commission"—the call to share the gospel with the whole world. That's a daunting assignment, but through the Holy Trinity, we are given everything we need. The Holy Spirit will comfort us through the work and cheer us on as we pursue it.

This Pentecost, turn to your Creator, the Father, in thanksgiving for all that you have been given. Call on Jesus, the Son, to impart his love and mercy to you. And count on the Holy Spirit, your Comforter and Advocate, to carry you through each day. The Lord doesn't expect you to make disciples of all nations (or your corner of the world) overnight. Just as you did at the beginning of the Lenten season, start small. Start with you.

- What is your relationship with the Holy Spirit? Do you feel as if you know the Holy Spirit as well as you know God the Father and God the Son?

April

THE HOLY SPIRIT, THE HOLY EUCHARIST, AND THE RESURRECTION

April is packed with new life and new possibilities. In addition to celebrating the resurrection, the Church dedicates April to the Holy Spirit and the Holy Eucharist. We are encouraged not only by the joyful witness of inspiring saints but also by the Holy Spirit's work in our lives and the spiritual nourishment of the Eucharist. April is full of life-sustaining potential.

Be sure to see the Lent and Easter section to round out your observance of April's special days.

Pray

Come, Holy Spirit

Come, Holy Spirit,
fill the hearts of your faithful,
and kindle in them the fire of your love.
Send forth your Spirit,
and they shall be created.
And you shall renew the face of the earth.

O God, who by the light of the Holy Spirit
did instruct the hearts of the faithful,
grant that by the same Holy Spirit
we may be truly wise and ever enjoy his consolations.
Through Christ our Lord. Amen.

An Act of Spiritual Communion

My Jesus,
I believe that you are present in the Most Holy Sacrament.
I love you above all things,
and I desire to receive you into my soul.
Since I cannot at this moment receive you sacramentally,
come at least spiritually into my heart.
I embrace you as if you were already there
and unite myself wholly to you.
Never permit me to be separated from you. Amen.

—St. Alphonsus Liguori

Liturgical Color

Purple in Lent
White in the Easter season

A Peek into April's Possibilities

(Be sure to see "Lent and Easter" for more.)

APRIL 2
Optional Memorial of St. Francis of Paola

APRIL 16
Optional Memorial of St. Bernadette

APRIL 25
Feast of St. Mark the Evangelist

APRIL 28
Optional Memorial of St. Gianna Beretta Molla

APRIL 29
Memorial of St. Catherine of Siena

April 2

ST. FRANCIS OF PAOLA
(1416–1507)

Hermit, founder of the Order of Minims; patron of seamen

Have you ever longed to be a hermit? If you're an introvert, you've probably felt the tug. In the whirlwind of life, there are times when many of us fantasize about getting away, *all alone*. Francis of Paola would understand.

Born in Paola, Italy, Francis became a hermit at the age of fifteen after receiving an education from the Franciscans. Despite his desire for solitude, Francis attracted followers who admired his humility, contemplative nature, ability to prophesy, and devotion to God. As his following grew, Francis—who was never ordained—established a rule for his disciples, built a monastery, and named his order the Hermits of St. Francis of Assisi. He later changed the order's name to the Minim Friars, to emphasize being the lowest or least (*minimi*) of God's followers.

Known for his gifts of prayer and healing, this hermit began an active life of ministry. As God repeatedly called him to service, especially as a champion of the poor, Francis set aside his personal desire to pray in solitude and attended to whatever God put in front of him.

At first glance, it seems as if Francis didn't have the privilege of living the life he had chosen. Yet God used Francis' gifts of deep prayer and contemplation to strengthen him for active work in the world when the time for that came. He was not extensively educated, and many said that when Francis offered counsel, his wisdom seemed to flow straight from God.

Nothing, including his years of prayerful solitude, was wasted in Francis' life. Every gift the Lord gave him prepared him for the next step.

- Have you ever felt that God was using a time in your life as preparation for a new stage? How did you handle that time of preparation? What difference did your preparation make when you reached that new stage?

Be lovers of peace, the most precious treasure that anyone can desire. . . . Live in such a way that you bring upon yourselves the blessing of God, and that the peace of God our Father may be with you always.

—St. Francis of Paola[42]

April 16

ST. BERNADETTE SOUBIROUS
(1844–1879)

Visionary, religious; patron of the ill, of those ridiculed for their faith, of shepherds, of the town of Lourdes in France, and against poverty

At the age of fourteen, Bernadette had a series of visions in which Mary asked that penance be done for the conversion of sinners, that a chapel be built at the grotto in which she appeared, and that pilgrimages take place to the site. When Bernadette asked who she was, Mary referred to herself as the Immaculate Conception, a term unknown to Bernadette. (The dogma of the Immaculate Conception had only recently been defined and had not filtered down to the poorly educated Bernadette.)

Bernadette's family lived in desperate poverty, she was often sick, and no one thought of her as particularly gifted. Civil and Church authorities considered her unreliable and repeatedly discounted and ridiculed her and her story. Steadfast, Bernadette maintained that she had seen and heard "the Immaculate Conception" on eighteen occasions.

Remarkable healings began to take place at the grotto, the authorities eventually capitulated, and Lourdes has since become a destination for pilgrims from throughout the world.

For her part, Bernadette refused to benefit in any way from the apparitions, turning down money and gifts and, later in life, giving up writing letters when she discovered those were considered special by the recipients.

Bernadette joined the Sisters of Charity in Nevers when she was twenty, becoming Sr. Marie-Bernard. The sisters did not always live up to their order's name. Many of them treated Bernadette cruelly, calling her lazy and assigning to her the most menial chores and responsibilities.

In spite of an endless battle with a variety of illnesses—including asthma, cholera, digestive struggles, and possibly bone cancer later in her short life—Bernadette courageously offered everything, including her physical suffering, to God. Deep ongoing prayer sustained her, and she exercised heroic humility in accepting whatever her fellow nuns threw her way. She died at the age of thirty-five. Her final words were "Blessed Mary, Mother of God, pray for me! A poor sinner, a poor sinner . . ."

- Bernadette once said of her encounters with Mary: "How I love to recall those sweet moments when I was beheld in eyes so full of kindness and mercy."[43] In those moments, Bernadette felt truly "seen," loved as a child of God worthy of every good thing. When have you felt "beheld in eyes . . . full of kindness and mercy," seen for who you truly are? Who has seen you that way?

O Mary, Mother of sorrows, at the foot of the cross you became our mother. I am a child of your sorrows, a child of Calvary. Let my heart be united to the cross, to the passion of Jesus Christ, and teach me not to be afraid of my own trials and crosses.

—St. Bernadette[44]

April 25

FEAST OF ST. MARK THE EVANGELIST

Connect

Our main source of information about Mark, who died sometime around AD 70, is the New Testament, both his Gospel and the Acts of the Apostles. In Acts 12:12 we read, "When he [Peter] realized this, he went to the house of Mary, the mother of John who is called Mark, where there were many people gathered in prayer."

This "John Mark" is thought to be a cousin of St. Barnabas and a disciple of Peter, with whom he had a close relationship. He accompanied Barnabas and Paul on various missionary journeys. His Gospel, probably written in Rome, is believed to be source material for both Matthew's and Luke's Gospels.

Some traditions hold that Mark became the first bishop at Alexandria, Egypt, but this isn't known for certain. Scholars also debate whether he actually crossed paths with Jesus. His remains are believed to be in the basilica in Venice; thus, he is the patron of Venice, as well as of lawyers and notaries.

To Ponder or Do

- The Gospel of Mark contains a powerful moment that we could ponder every day but particularly on the feast of this great Evangelist:

Now Jesus and his disciples set out for the villages of Caesarea Philippi. Along the way he asked his disciples, "Who do people say that I am?" They said in reply, "John the Baptist, others Elijah, still others one of the prophets." And he asked them, "But who do you say that I am?" Peter said to him in reply, "You are the Messiah." (Mark 8:27-29)

- Pause and ask yourself, "Who do I say that Jesus is?"

- As you celebrate St. Mark the Evangelist today, consider these words from Pope Francis:

[I]t is not the same thing to have known Jesus as not to have known him, not the same thing to walk with him as to walk blindly, not the same thing to hear his word as not to know it, and not the same thing to contemplate him, to worship him, to find our peace in him, as not to. It is not the same thing to try to build the world with his Gospel as to try to do so by our own lights. We know well that with Jesus life becomes richer and that with him it is easier to find meaning in everything. This is why we evangelize. (*Evangelii Gaudium*, 266)[45]

• Take a moment to pray with these words from St. Augustine:

Do not grieve or complain that you were born in a time when you can no longer see God in the flesh. He did not in fact take this privilege from you. As he says: "Whatever you have done to the least of my brothers, you did to me."[46]

Pray

Lord, we all have to answer the question "Who do you say that I am?" Let me answer it every day with faith and conviction, knowing that you are the Messiah, the Son of God, my Savior.

April 28

ST. GIANNA BERETTA MOLLA
(1922–1962)

Wife and mother, physician; patron of wives, mothers, doctors, families, unborn children, and the town of Magenta, Italy

Gianna was born into an active, devout family, and she readily embraced her Catholic faith throughout her life—a life she ultimately sacrificed in order to best serve her child.

Gianna wondered if she had a calling to religious life, so she made a pilgrimage to Lourdes to pray and discern God's will. When she returned, she met Pietro Molla and fell in love; she felt God had clearly answered her questions and prayers. They married in 1955, when she was thirty-three, and had three children, followed by two miscarriages. Gianna pursued her career as a pediatric doctor, was active in Catholic Action and the St. Vincent de Paul Society, and was a daily communicant.

In 1961, when Gianna was pregnant with their sixth child, her doctor discovered a tumor in her uterus. She was advised to have a total hysterectomy. But Gianna would allow the doctors to remove only the tumor, thus preserving the baby's life. Several months later the Mollas' daughter was born. A week after that, Gianna died of septic peritonitis.

Gianna Molla was beatified on April 24, 1994, and canonized on May 16, 2004. In his canonization homily, Pope John Paul II said,

> [T]his holy mother of a family remained heroically faithful to the commitment she made on the day of her marriage. The extreme sacrifice she sealed with her life testifies that only those who have the courage to give of themselves totally to God and to others are able to fulfil themselves.[47]

- As Jesus said, "This is my commandment: love one another as I love you. No one has greater love than this, to lay down one's life for one's friends" (John 15:12-13). Most of us will not face such extreme choices, but ask yourself, "In what other ways am I called to lay down my life for the people I love?"

Jesus, I love you. Jesus, I love you.

—St. Gianna, as she was dying[48]

April 29

ST. CATHERINE OF SIENA
(1347–1380)

Lay Dominican, mystic, author, Doctor of the Church; copatron of Italy and Europe and of nurses

Catherine was a study in contradictions. A mystic who as a child shut herself in her room to pray, fast, plunge into contemplation, and emerge only for Mass, she was also charismatic, charming, a joy to be around, and, as a young woman, full of practical and spiritual advice for everyone from the poor to princes to popes.

Her parents wanted her to marry, but Catherine had other plans. She said she had her first mystical vision at age six—she saw the Lord sitting on a throne, with saints all around him—and knew she wanted to spend her life with Jesus. As a teen she became a Third Order Dominican, cared for the poor, and grew in mystical gifts. In one vision, she saw herself being espoused to Christ; he presented her with a magnificent ring that she alone could see. Her holiness was palpable, sometimes actually visible to others, as when they witnessed her ecstasies and her gift of tears.

Catherine had difficulty learning to read and didn't learn to write until a couple of years before she died. Yet she engaged in extensive correspondence—dictating her letters—with political and religious figures, advising and even admonishing them when she saw a need for correction or exhortation. When the Western, or Papal, Schism occurred and there were ostensibly two and later even three popes, Catherine devoted herself to healing the Church. Pope Benedict XVI said at a general audience in November 2010,

> When the fame of her holiness spread, she became the protagonist of an intense activity of spiritual guidance for people from every walk of life: nobles and politicians, artists and ordinary people, consecrated men and women and religious, including Pope Gregory XI who was living at Avignon in that period and whom she energetically and effectively urged to return to Rome.[49]

Catherine of Siena is the author of *The Dialogue*, a mystical memoir written in the form of a conversation between God and a soul striving for holiness. Like other saints who seem to "do it all," she shows us that contemplative prayer and active ministry can go hand in hand and that faith calls for honesty and courage.

Catherine died in Rome at the age of thirty-three. In 1970 Pope Paul VI declared her a Doctor of the Church.

- Saints who had visions of God as children can be intimidating, setting the bar a little too high. But Catherine lived very much in the world, spreading God's love through active service. She would want us to do the same while remaining true to our unique personalities. A popular quote attributed to her says, "Be who God meant you to be, and you will set the world on fire."

  You don't have to try to be St. Catherine or anyone else. Just ask God who he wants you to be.

And I promise you that I shall be with you always, and be of much more use to you on the other side than I ever could be here on earth, for then I shall have left the darkness behind me and move in the eternal light.

—St. Catherine of Siena to her disciples,
just before her death[50]

May

THE BLESSED
VIRGIN MARY

May is the month of Mary. Of course, she is ever present in our faith, but the Church sets aside certain times of the year—particularly May and October—to encourage us to dig a little deeper, perhaps reexamine old habits or establish new avenues of communication with our Mother, Mary. And how fitting it is that we should honor Mary in May, when we are also still celebrating Easter.

Mary endured the worst and most bitter torture a mother could endure as she witnessed the death of her son. But now she has seen the resurrection. He is risen! His mother played an extraordinary role in the sanctifying and redemptive work of Jesus Christ.

Pray

Mother Mary, you endured so much as you walked this earth. Though you were without sin, you weren't without emotion. From tremendous suffering to unspeakable joy, you know and understand the ups and downs of our days, the difficult and unpredictable nature of life. For the enormous and the minuscule issues, from the mundane to the profound, pray for me, Mother Mary.

Liturgical Color

White when still celebrating the great fifty days of Easter, extended to include Trinity Sunday (the Sunday after Pentecost) and the Solemnity of the Most Holy Body and Blood of Christ (the second Sunday after Pentecost)
Green when we've returned to Ordinary Time

A Peek into May's Possibilities

(Be sure to see "Lent and Easter" for more.)

MAY 1
Optional Memorial of St. Joseph the Worker

MAY 13
Optional Memorial of Our Lady of Fatima

MAY 22
Optional Memorial of St. Rita of Cascia

MAY 25
Optional Memorial of St. Bede the Venerable

MAY 26
Memorial of St. Philip Neri

MAY 30
Optional Memorial of St. Joan of Arc

MAY 31
Feast of the Visitation of the Blessed Virgin Mary

May 1

ST. JOSEPH THE WORKER

Connect

Husband of Mary, foster father of Jesus, and provider for the Holy Family, Joseph is also a patron of workers and laborers—a man we can always honor and celebrate. Pope Pius XII instituted this feast day in 1955 to highlight the value of our everyday labors in our families, in the workplace, and in our service to God.

In *Redemptoris Custos*, his apostolic exhortation honoring St. Joseph, Pope John Paul II said,

> Work was the daily expression of love in the life of the Family of Nazareth. The Gospel specifies the kind of work Joseph did in order to support his family: he was a carpenter. This simple word sums up Joseph's entire life. . . . Human work, and especially manual labor, receive special prominence in the Gospel. Along with the humanity of the Son of God, work too has been taken up in the mystery of the Incarnation, and has

also been redeemed in a special way. At the workbench where he plied his trade together with Jesus, Joseph brought human work closer to the mystery of the Redemption.[51]

Do you see your work as holy? Whether you're single or married, lay or religious, working inside or outside your home, a mother, a father—know that everything you do is a holy action when you do it for God. Laundry, going to the office, cooking, teaching online classes, picking up takeout, putting in a twelve-hour shift at the hospital, walking the floor at 4 a.m. with a baby, working toward your degree—all are valuable work, and all are steps on the climb to heaven. Remind yourself that your labor—your "daily expression of love"—has meaning.

To Ponder or Do

- Did you have time to celebrate St. Joseph in March? If March was crazy, here's another chance to honor this marvelous saint. It's never too late to grab cream puffs from the bakery, a bouquet of flowers from the grocery store, and create a simple St. Joseph's Table.

- Pray the prayer below, and remind yourself that work, even the most menial of tasks, is a gift from and for God—a series of actions that become holy when we offer them for him.

- Do you keep a journal? If so, take a few minutes to make a note of the ways in which your work has served, blessed, or changed someone else this week.

Pray

Glorious St. Joseph, patron of all who are devoted to toil, obtain for me the grace to toil in the spirit of penance, in order thereby to atone for my many sins; to toil conscientiously, putting devotion to duty before my own inclinations; to labor with thankfulness and joy, deeming it an honor to employ and to develop, by my labor, the gifts I have received from Almighty God; to work with order, peace, moderation, and patience without ever shrinking from weariness and difficulties; to work above all with a pure intention and with detachment from self, having always before my eyes the hour of death and the accounting which I must then render of time ill spent, of talents unemployed, of good undone, and of my empty pride in success, which is so fatal to the work of God.

All for Jesus, all through Mary, all in imitation of you, O Patriarch Joseph! This shall be my motto in life and in death. Amen.
    —Prayer of Pope Pius X to Joseph, Patron of Workers [52]

May 13

MEMORIAL OF OUR LADY OF FATIMA

Connect

In 1917 Mary appeared in Fatima, Portugal, to three children—Jacinta and Francisco Marto and Lucia dos Santos—over the course of several months. Her message was simple: pray the Rosary for sinners, and pray for peace. It might be hard to relate to the idea of receiving a vision of Mary, but it's easy to relate to the message she gave the children. We can all pray for sinners, including ourselves, for the world, and for peace. As Pope John Paul II said in his 1982 homily on this feast day, "The message of Fatima is, in its fundamental nucleus, a call to conversion and repentance, as in the Gospel."

To Ponder or Do

- Spend some time reflecting on the challenge of every Christian: the call to ongoing conversion. That's the simple but profound message behind each and every apparition of Mary. Pope Francis said,

God is patient with each of us: he does not tire, he does not desist after our "no"; he leaves us free even to distance ourselves from him and to make mistakes. Thinking about God's patience is wonderful! How the Lord always waits for us; he is always beside us to help us; but he respects our freedom. And he anxiously awaits our "yes," so as to welcome us anew in his fatherly arms and to fill us with his boundless mercy. Faith in God asks us to renew every day the choice of good over evil, the choice of the truth rather than lies, the choice of love for our neighbor over selfishness.[53]

- Ask yourself, "What can I do today to further my own conversion? What, if anything, is holding me back from taking a new step?"

- Pray the Rosary, a decade of the Rosary, or a Hail Mary for worldwide conversion and peace. Don't be hard on yourself if you don't have time for a full Rosary today; every prayer counts.

- Read Pope Francis' entire prayer to Our Lady of Fatima from his visit to Portugal on May 12, 2017. You can find it on the Vatican website under Pope Francis, travel, 2017. See excerpt below, with link to the full prayer in the endnote.

Pray

Show us the strength of your protective mantle.
In your Immaculate Heart,

be the refuge of sinners
and the way that leads to God.

In union with my brothers and sisters,
in faith, in hope and in love,
I entrust myself to you.
In union with my brothers and sisters, through you, I
consecrate myself to God,
O Virgin of the Rosary of Fatima.

And at last, enveloped in the Light that comes from your
hands,
I will give glory to the Lord for ever and ever. Amen.

> —From Pope Francis' prayer to Our Lady of Fatima,
> May 2017[54]

May 22

ST. RITA OF CASCIA (1381–1457)

Wife, mother, religious, mystic; patron of impossible causes,
difficult marriages, parenthood, widows, the sick,
those with wounds

Rita, born in Roccaporena, Italy, felt the call to religious
life as a child but succumbed to parental pressure to

marry. Her husband was a cruel, violent man who mistreated and belittled her, was unfaithful to her, and raised their two sons to follow in his footsteps. When he was killed in a fight, his sons swore revenge but fell ill and died before they could carry out their plans. It's said that while they were sick, Rita may have convinced them to repent of their past ways and forgive the people who had killed their father.

After her husband's death, Rita was free to follow her childhood calling. Initially rejected by the Augustinians because she was a widow, the order eventually relaxed that rule and allowed Rita to enter. She was unfailingly prayerful, loving, and devoted to God and everyone who surrounded her. She offered tender care for her fellow nuns when they were sick.

Rita was passionately devoted to the passion of Christ. When mysterious wounds appeared on her forehead, they were believed to be a mystical manifestation of Christ's crown of thorns. She bore the wounds for the final fifteen years of her life.

- Staying in an abusive situation is not the lesson to take away from Rita's life. Not at all—no one should remain in an abusive situation. There are no easy answers here, but Rita is a heavenly advocate for those who are in distress. Pray today, with St. Rita, for women in abusive marriages, that they find hope, healing, and genuine solutions. Consider making a donation to an organization that offers aid to women in distress.

Holy patron of those in need, St. Rita, so humble, so pure and patient, whose pleadings with your Divine Spouse are so irresistible, obtain for me from our crucified Christ my request. Be kind to me, for the greater glory of God.

— Prayer to St. Rita of Cascia[55]

PILGRIMAGE ALERT

The National Shrine of St. Rita of Cascia is located in Philadelphia and is operated by the Augustinian Province of St. Thomas of Villanova. For more information, visit saintritashrine.org.

May 25

ST. BEDE THE VENERABLE
(673–735)

Priest, Doctor of the Church

An outstanding yet humble scholar, Bede's magnum opus was *The Ecclesiastical History of the English People*, a work of immense historical value. He's called "the Father of English History." He was a translator and commentator of Scripture, a poet, and a biographer of saints. He also wrote commentaries on history, philosophy, and the sciences.

At the age of seven, Bede went to live and be educated in a monastery in Jarrow, England, and he never left, other than for a possible foray to York to teach for a short time. While his life could be called geographically narrow, his extraordinary influence extended, and continues to extend, to the entire world.

Bede was more than an academic however. He had an affinity for the laity and an understanding of the average person's thirst for holiness. Though it was basically unheard of at the time, he recommended that some should be allowed to receive Holy Communion every week or perhaps even daily.

Pope Leo XIII declared St. Bede a Doctor of the Church in 1899. Pope Francis chose his motto, *Miserando atque eligendo*, from a homily of St. Bede that refers to Jesus' call of St. Matthew. The motto can be translated, "He saw him through the eyes of mercy and chose him."

- Sometimes we overlook the fact that our talents and skills are gifts that can serve others, not simply things we like to do. What talents has God given you for his glory and the care of others?

It has ever been my delight to learn or teach or write.

—St. Bede the Venerable[56]

May 26

ST. PHILIP NERI (1515–1595)

*Priest, missionary, mystic, founder of the order of the
Oratorians; patron of Rome, of Special Forces,
of joy and humor*

Picture the most affable, lovable, humorous, and genuinely holy priest you know. He's probably a lot like St. Philip Neri. Everything we know of Philip tells us that he was an appealing mix of popular and pious. And while he was serious about his holiness, he was able to see the joy and humor in everything.

Life as a businessman was decidedly not for Philip, so he left his uncle's business and headed to Rome, trusting entirely that God would help him figure out how to fill his empty pockets. He found work as a tutor, studied philosophy and theology, and fueled everything he did with prayer.

Philip started a street ministry of sorts—unusual at the time—won many converts, and attracted numerous followers, who helped him serve the poor. He gathered people for prayer, discussion, and even picnics, musical performances, and pilgrimage trips. Philip's methods of evangelization seemed so unorthodox that Pope Paul IV put a stop to them for a time, but the succeeding Pius IV allowed Philip to continue. Eventually, these gatherings formed the basis for the Congregation of the Oratory of St. Philip Neri.

St. Philip was known for his big heart, figuratively speaking, but a mystical experience in 1544 apparently enlarged his heart physically as well. While in prayer on the eve of Pentecost, Philip saw a globe of fire enter his mouth. It settled in his heart, and ever after Philip had a swelling over his heart as well as heart palpitations that shook his entire body when he spoke of the love of God. An autopsy confirmed that two of his ribs had broken and formed a curved arch around the saint's heart.

In 1551 Philip was ordained a priest. He continued to attract followers. His biographer, Fr. Pietro Giacomo Bacci, compared the attraction to a magnet drawing iron. He wrote, in *The Life of St. Philip Neri*,

> When he was called upon to be merry, he was so; if there was a demand upon his sympathy, he was equally ready. He gave the same welcome to all, caressing the poor equally with the rich, and laboring in the service of all to the utmost limits of his power. In consequence of his being so accessible, and so ready to receive all comers, many went to him every day, and some continued for the space of thirty, nay forty years.[57]

Pope Francis noted on the fifth centenary of Philip's birth:

> His mission as "chiseler of souls" was certainly helped by the unique attractive force of his person, distinguished by human warmth, joy, meekness, and gentleness. These particular attributes of his originated in the ardent experience of Christ and in the action of the Divine Spirit who expanded his heart.[58]

- Some people just seem to have it all: holiness, happiness, and a magnetism that draws others to God. Do you know anyone like this? If so, what impact have they made on you?

Scruples and melancholy, stay away from my house.

—St. Philip Neri [59]

May 30

ST. JOAN OF ARC (1412–1431)

Mystic, military leader; patron of soldiers and France

Joan was an uneducated teenage peasant who led the French in decisive victories against British occupying troops during the Hundred Years War. Born in Domrémy, she began hearing the voices of St. Michael, St. Catherine of Alexandria, and St. Margaret of Antioch urging her to save her country. After three years of seeing visions and hearing voices, Joan appealed to authorities and won support to lead the French army on a mission, acting as a spiritual leader, even encouraging all to go to Confession before battle.

Joan was initially successful, but after several defeats in battle, she was captured and turned over to the English. She came to trial before the bishop of Cauchon on a variety of charges, including witchcraft and heresy. King Charles VII, whose cause she had championed and who owed his crowning to her, did nothing to help her as she was persecuted by men of the Church.

Joan's faith in God was striking. She told the tribunal, "You say that you are my judge; I do not know if you are; but take good heed not to judge me ill, because you would put yourself in great peril. And I warn you so that if God punish you for it I shall have done my duty in telling you." When further questioned about this peril, she replied that St. Catherine had assured her of help and victory and had told her, "Take everything peacefully: have no care for your martyrdom; in the end you shall come to the Kingdom of Paradise."

Joan's accusers challenged this as arrogance. They asked if she thought she was incapable of mortal sin. Joan confidently replied, "I do not know; but in everything I commit myself to God."[60]

Joan retained her steadfast faith and courage until the end. She was burned at the stake when she was just nineteen years old. Mark Twain, who was known for his acerbic wit and often scathing social commentary and who was no fan of the Catholic Church, was so captivated by Joan's story that he wrote a sincere and earnest novel about her, considering it his best work.

In a general audience on January 26, 2011, Pope Benedict XVI said,

In Jesus Joan contemplated the whole reality of the Church, the "Church triumphant" of Heaven, as well as the "Church militant" on earth. According to her words, "About Jesus Christ and the Church, I simply know they're just one thing." This affirmation, cited in the *Catechism of the Catholic Church* (795), has a truly heroic character in the context of the *Trial of Condemnation*, before her judges, men of the Church who were persecuting and condemning her. In the Love of Jesus, Joan found the strength to love the Church to the very end, even at the moment she was sentenced.[61]

Joan was canonized in 1920 and is a model of heroic virtue and integrity.

Joan of Arc is a larger-than-life figure who continues to inspire us despite our difficulty in relating to her circumstances. "I do not fear the soldiers," Joan said before she went to battle, "for my road is made open to me; and if the soldiers come, I have God, my Lord, who will know how to clear the route that leads to the Dauphin. It is for this that I was born."[62] This is popularly shortened to the inspirational "I am not afraid, for God is with me. I was born to do this."

- Pope Benedict XVI pointed out that Joan was treated unconscionably by the very men who should have been helping her. Have you ever had to separate a fallible Catholic's actions from the divine nature of the Catholic Church? What helped you through the experience? We can ask St. Joan to pray for us when we struggle with issues in today's Church.

I entrust myself to God my Creator, I love him with my whole heart.

—St. Joan of Arc[63]

May 31

FEAST OF THE VISITATION OF THE BLESSED VIRGIN MARY

Connect

Among the numerous beautiful truths we witness in Mary's visit to her cousin Elizabeth, a simple one shines through: these two women were ready to take care of and serve one another. Each woman experienced a pregnancy in unusual circumstances, to say the least, which might drive anyone to withdraw to take care of her own needs. Instead, these two reached out to one another. In their meeting—highlighted by the fact that Elizabeth's child "leapt for joy" at the sound of Mary's greeting (Luke 1:44)—Mary and Elizabeth found joy, gratitude, and hope for the future.

To Ponder or Do

- Read the Canticle of Mary (Luke 1:46-55). Then pray a decade of the Rosary, focusing on the second Joyful Mystery, the Visitation.

- As you read these words from Pope John Paul II, consider what you can do to "arise" and "start moving."

What might work—or not work—as you strive to bring Christ's light to others?

In describing Mary's departure for Judea, the Evangelist uses the verb "anístemi," which means "to arise," "to start moving." Considering that this verb is used in the Gospels to indicate Jesus' Resurrection (cf. Mk 8:31; 9:9, 31; Lk 24:7, 46) or physical actions that imply a spiritual effort (Lk 5:27-28; 15:18, 20), we can suppose that Luke wishes to stress with this expression the vigorous zeal which led Mary, under the inspiration of the Holy Spirit, to give the world its Savior. . . .

Mary's visit to Elizabeth, in fact, is a prelude to Jesus' mission and, in cooperating from the beginning of her motherhood in the Son's redeeming work, she becomes the model for those in the Church who set out to bring Christ's light and joy to the people of every time and place.

—Pope John Paul II[64]

- Do you know a woman who could use a "visitation"? Or maybe you're the one in need. Call a friend, send a text, write a note, or schedule a get-together. Drop off a treat, a gift, or a bottle of your friend's favorite wine. If it's someone you haven't seen for a while, let her know you want to get regular "visitations" back on the calendar.

  We women need each other! Our visits may not be three months long, as was Mary's to Elizabeth, but let's not neglect the power of female friendship to buoy our spirits and keep us going.

Pray

Lord, your word offers us examples of beautiful and meaningful friendships among strong, faithful women. Thank you for showing me the power of feminine support in my life. Help me nourish and build the kind of friendships that will help me grow continually closer to you.

June

THE SACRED HEART

After the intensity of Lenten preparations and a joyful, extended celebration of Easter, it's time for some "ordinary living" in Ordinary Time. As we noted earlier, "Ordinary Time" actually refers to the days of the liturgical calendar that are "ordered," or numbered, in the absence of a great or preparatory liturgical season. Lent and Easter have strengthened us and led to renewal, so what's next in the spotlight? Devotion to the Sacred Heart of Jesus.

The Solemnity of the Sacred Heart of Jesus is a moveable feast that falls on the Friday after the second Sunday after Pentecost. Devotion to the Sacred Heart is one of the most widespread and popular of all devotions in the Church. St. Margaret Mary Alacoque had visions of the Sacred Heart of Jesus in the late seventeenth century, and the devotion has endured. According to the saint, Jesus made twelve promises to those who would honor him with this devotion:

1. I will give them all the graces necessary in their state of life.
2. I will establish peace in their homes.
3. I will comfort them in all their afflictions.
4. I will be their secure refuge during life, and above all, in death.
5. I will bestow abundant blessings upon all their undertakings.
6. Sinners will find in my heart the source and infinite ocean of mercy.
7. Lukewarm souls shall become fervent.
8. Fervent souls shall quickly mount to high perfection.
9. I will bless every place in which an image of my heart is exposed and honored.

10. I will give to priests the gift of touching the most hardened hearts.
11. Those who shall promote this devotion shall have their names written in my heart.
12. I promise you in the excessive mercy of my heart that my all-powerful love will grant to all those who receive Holy Communion on the First Fridays in nine consecutive months the grace of final persever-ance; they shall not die in my disgrace, nor without receiving their sacraments. My divine heart shall be their safe refuge in this last moment.[65]

Pray

Lord, please let your divine and sacred heart be my safe refuge, not only in my final days but every day of my life.

Liturgical Color

Green, for Ordinary Time (after white for Trinity Sunday
and Solemnity of the Most Holy Body and Blood of Christ)

A Peek into June's Possibilities

JUNE 5
Memorial of St. Boniface

JUNE 9
Optional Memorial of St. Ephrem

JUNE 13
Memorial of St. Anthony of Padua

JUNE 21
Memorial of St. Aloysius Gonzaga

JUNE 24
Solemnity of the Birth of St. John the Baptist

JUNE 29
Solemnity of Sts. Peter and Paul

June 5

ST. BONIFACE (C. 675–754)

Bishop, martyr; patron of Germany, tailors, brewers

This Englishman's given name was Winfred, but Pope Gregory II was so pleased with his missionary work that he dubbed him Boniface, "he who performs good works." Known as the apostle of the Germans, Boniface was a scholarly Benedictine monk who chose to leave academic life for the challenge of mission work among people practicing pagan religions. One story tells of Boniface chopping down "Thor's Oak" in an effort to prove that the pagan deity held no sway. People expected the gods to swiftly fell Boniface, but the gods failed to strike, and thus Boniface won many converts.

Boniface also had to deal with lackadaisical, uneducated, and uncaring clergy in the region. He labored to restore meaningful obedience of priests to their bishops, and he was responsible for establishing numerous monasteries of devout religious who spread Christ's word through prayer, education, and culture. He became the archbishop of Germany in 732 and later worked on Church reform in France as well.

Boniface died in 754 while on a mission trip to Friesland, the site of his first missionary efforts. He and fifty-three companions, waiting for Confirmation candidates to arrive, were murdered by pagans. Boniface, who was reading the Gospels when he was attacked, calmly told those with him not to fear dying for their faith.

The priest Willibald collected the facts of Boniface's life from his disciples and wrote a short biography within ten years of Boniface's martyrdom. This work can be found online.[66]

- Boniface shows us that some things never change: there will always be a need for conversion, both within and outside the Church. Rather than be discouraged by that, we can aspire to also be one "who performs good works." What one good work can you do today?

The Church is like a great ship being pounded by the waves of life's different stresses. Our duty is not to abandon ship, but to keep her on her course.

—St. Boniface[67]

June 9

ST. EPHREM (C. 306–373)

Deacon, Doctor of the Church;
patron of spiritual directors and spiritual leaders

Dubbed the "Harp of the Holy Spirit" for his musical genius and poetic hymns, Ephrem—teacher, poet, and deacon who composed homilies in verse—is credited with introducing song into public worship. Pope Benedict XVI said, "It is the fact that theology and poetry converge in his work which makes it so special. If we desire to approach his doctrine, we must insist on this from the outset: namely, on the fact that he produces theology in poetical form."[68]

This humble poet wanted a simple life and had no desire to become a priest. One story says that he escaped what would have been repugnant to him—becoming a bishop—by pretending to be insane. Ephrem knew he could best share the faith through his writing, which was universally embraced as insightful and arresting. He wasn't above a little subversive evangelization either: he was known to borrow the melodies of heretical groups and compose transcendent, orthodox lyrics to accompany them, transforming heresy into heavenly praise.

When Pope Benedict XV declared Ephrem a Doctor of the Church in 1920, he said, "In all of [his writings], his purity of soul shines forth as a 'burning and shining' evangelical lamp. By illustrating the truth, he makes us love and embrace it."[69]

- While no one would recommend faking madness to dodge a demand, Ephrem knew best how to put his talents to use. Have you identified your greatest God-given talent? Have you ever wanted to dodge outside demands and put your skills to use in a different way?

How can my harp, O Lord, cease to praise you?
How could I teach my tongue infidelity?
—St. Ephrem, "The Harp of the Spirit"[70]

In your bread hides the Spirit who cannot be consumed; in your wine is the fire that cannot be swallowed. The Spirit in your bread, fire in your wine: behold a wonder heard from our lips.
— St. Ephrem, Hymn *De Fide*[71]

June 13

ST. ANTHONY OF PADUA
(1195–1231)

Priest and Doctor of the Church; patron of lost items, lost people, lost souls, stolen articles, amputees, travelers

"It's lost?"

"Yeah. I have no idea where I left it."

"Pray to St. Anthony. It always works."

Such conversations probably happen often in Catholic households—perhaps in yours. Anthony is the patron saint of lost things, and I know I'm not the only Catholic who asks him to intercede for me. And the item turns up, often in a place I have already looked.

Born Fernando Martins, this saint took a bit of time to find his place in the world. He joined the Augustinian order when he was fifteen and developed such a deep knowledge of the Bible that he was nicknamed the "Repository of Scripture."

After several years, moved by the sacrifice of some Franciscan martyrs, Fernando received permission to join the Franciscan order, taking the name Anthony. On his first missionary trip, he fell ill and was then assigned to a hermitage, where he studied Scripture and led a quiet life of routine chores and prayer. His career as a preacher happened as if by accident. And isn't that how the Holy Spirit's work often appears?

When no one else was available to speak at an ordination, the superior drafted Anthony at the last minute. He so astounded everyone with his knowledge of the Bible and his eloquent, simple delivery that the Franciscans immediately sent him out to preach. He drew such enormous crowds that, on occasion, a bodyguard had to protect him from eager followers.

St. Francis of Assisi personally approved Anthony's assignment as the theology teacher to the Franciscans. Anthony settled in Padua after being named the provincial superior of northern Italy. He died there at the age of thirty-five.

St. Anthony's patronage of lost articles may be rooted in an actual incident, though the circumstances have probably been embellished. A novice took Anthony's book of psalms with him when he quit the order. The book was treasured not only as Scripture but for the marginalia Anthony had scribbled in it. Anthony prayed for the book to be returned, and it's said that God answered the prayer and even one-upped the saint: the novice returned the book and returned to the order too.

Anthony was declared a Doctor of the Church in 1946.

- In his Fifteenth Sermon after Pentecost, St. Anthony made a timeless point:

Do you want to have God always in your mind? Be just as he made you to be. Do not go seeking another "you." Do not make yourself otherwise than he made you. Then you will always have God in mind.

—St. Anthony of Padua[72]

Do you ever feel lost? Ask St. Anthony to help you find the "you" God created you to be.

If things created are so full of loveliness, how resplendent with beauty must be he who made them! The wisdom of the worker is apparent in his handiwork.

—St. Anthony of Padua[73]

June 21

ST. ALOYSIUS GONZAGA
(1568–1591)

Religious; patron of Catholic students and youth, especially Jesuit students

The Gonzagas, a ruling family in northern Italy, weren't known for their high moral standards, but somehow, in the midst of courtly decadence, a saint was born. From the age of seven, Aloysius displayed a deep level of piety, much to his father's consternation. The senior Gonzaga wanted his son to be a star in the military, but Aloysius treasured other plans.

By his early teens, Aloysius was praying in the middle of the night, fasting several times a week, and was determined to join the Jesuits. It took time, but in 1585, Aloysius finally convinced his father to let him relinquish his title and join the order.

In the Jesuit novitiate, Aloysius was finally in his element. Instead of creating his own extreme penances, he followed the direction of his superiors. If that meant fasting less than he used to or taking part in recreation time with his fellow seminarians when he'd rather be doing something more "spiritual," then he was ready. Like many a zealous soul, he learned that when it comes to the life of faith, obedience is often more important than personal preferences.

In 1591 Aloysius contracted the plague while caring for plague victims. His spiritual director and confessor, St. Robert Bellarmine, administered the Sacrament of the Anointing of the Sick before Aloysius died. He was only twenty-three.

Aloysius was canonized in 1726 by Pope Benedict XIII.

- Aloysius is an example of a devoted soul who was too hard on himself in his choices of penance. How do you approach penance? Do you think you are too hard or too easy on yourself? Or have you found the golden mean?

We are often moved with passion, and we think it to be zeal.

—St. Thomas à Kempis[74]

June 24

SOLEMNITY OF THE BIRTH OF JOHN THE BAPTIST

Connect

It took me a long time to connect with this celebration. I didn't feel an immediate kinship with John the Baptist. His extreme and zealous asceticism, his diet of locusts and honey. . . . My life is far removed from John's.

Eventually, I learned that "locusts" might refer to some sort of honey cake or carob bean, and that made John a little more relatable. On the other hand, it's entirely possible that when the Bible says "locusts," it means *locusts*. Obviously, I shouldn't rely on a dietary connection to find meaning in Scripture.

I finally connected with John the Baptist the day a particular Bible verse struck me in a new and profound way: "He must increase; I must decrease" (John 3:30). No wonder John is known as a great evangelizer. He gets right to the point.

I had read and heard this verse untold times and had always understood it to be an obvious acknowledgment of John's situation. But one day—who knows why; the Holy Spirit is tricky!—it pierced my soul. Christ must increase in *me; I* must decrease.

John wasn't talking only about himself and about the way his role would change and fade. He was offering words for *me* to live by too. John couldn't care less if I connected with *him*. He always pointed to Christ.

Our life as Christians is not about us. It's about Jesus, about allowing him to increase in our hearts, minds, and souls. And it's about becoming a clear window through which others can see Jesus, every day, in our words and actions.

To Ponder or Do

- Read about the birth of John in Luke 1:57-80. Verses 68-79 are called the "Canticle of Zechariah," a song of thanksgiving that John's father offered to the Lord. It is also known as the *Benedictus*, and it is recited daily as part of Lauds, or Morning Prayer, in the Liturgy of the Hours.

- Read *Evangelii Nuntiandi* [On Evangelization in the Modern World], the inspiring apostolic exhortation of Pope Paul VI. Rather than approaching evangelization as a grim responsibility, he advises us to

  preserve the delightful and comforting joy of evangelizing, even when it is in tears that we must sow. May it mean for us—as it did for John the Baptist, . . . and for a multitude of splendid evangelizers all through the Church's history—an interior enthusiasm that nobody and nothing can quench.[75]

  Consider your own efforts to share the faith. Where do you fall on the unquenchable-interior-enthusiasm spectrum?

- Plan a picnic, party, or get-together with friends, and light a bonfire to celebrate St. John the Baptist. Bonfires became a common way to observe John's birthday in the Middle Ages, as Christians adopted the summer solstice and "baptized" it with Christian observances such as this one. For kiddos, add snacks that represent "honey and locusts." A quick internet search for "Liturgical year food honey and locusts" will yield fun and easy results.

Pray

Lord, John the Baptist was so much more than a herald of your arrival. He was a model disciple who sought simplicity, holiness, repentance, and the spreading of your message. Help me every day to remember and live his words and example: "He must increase; I must decrease" (John 3:30).

June 29

STS. PETER AND PAUL

Connect

St. Peter: apostle, first to proclaim that
Jesus was the Messiah, first pope
St. Paul: dramatic convert, prolific writer,
preacher, evangelist extraordinaire

Though Sts. Peter and Paul may be known as towering figures, heroic martyrs, and cornerstones of the faith, they also displayed traits that we can all relate to. Both men were flawed human beings.

Pre-conversion Paul, who was known as Saul, was a Pharisee and a persecutor of Christ. His conversion—however sudden, dramatic, and complete—did not transform him into a perfect disciple immediately. Paul understood sin and the ways we can repeatedly and regrettably fall into it. As he said in Romans 7:15, "What I do, I do not understand. For I do not do what I want, but I do what I hate." One couldn't ask for a more humble and human admission.

Peter, for all his deep and genuine faith, wavered and doubted, as when he tried to walk on water to meet Jesus, faltered, and sank (see Matthew 14:22-33) and when he betrayed the Lord by denying him three times (see John 18:15-27). And yet this was the man Jesus chose to be the first "servant of the servants of God."

How heartening that God, from the very beginning, has given us role models with flaws: Moses, Jacob, David, and many others. They remind us that our Lord doesn't expect perfection right out of the gate. We are works in progress.

To Ponder or Do

- Spend some time with Scripture passages about Peter and Paul. Remind yourself that these men were real human beings, with real lives, relatable fears, and unforeseen challenges. In what ways do you relate to Peter or Paul? Do you embrace the truth that God loves you deeply, in spite of your flaws and mistakes?

- Pray with this verse: "Cast all your anxieties on him, for he cares about you" (1 Peter 5:7, RSVCE). Or this one: "I can do all things in him who strengthens me" (Philippians 4:13, RSVCE).

- Read Pope Francis' short homily from the Holy Mass and Blessing of the Sacred Pallium for the new Metropolitan Archbishops on the Solemnity of Sts. Peter and Paul, June 29, 2021, excerpted here with the full text at vatican.va. Ponder the focus on freedom. As Pope Francis said, *"Peter and Paul were free because they were set free."*

At the heart of their story is not their own gifts and abilities; at the center is the encounter with Christ that changed their lives. They experienced a love that healed them and set them free. They then became apostles and ministers of freedom for others. . . .

. . . Jesus did not judge them or humiliate them. Instead, he shared their life with affection and closeness. He supported them by his prayer, and even at times reproached them to make them change. To Peter, Jesus gently says: "I have prayed for you that your own faith may not fail" (Luke 22:32). And to Paul: "Saul, Saul, why do you persecute me?" (Acts 9:4). He does the same with us: he assures us of his closeness by praying and interceding for us before the Father, and gently reproaching us whenever we go astray, so that we can find the strength to arise and resume the journey.

We too have been touched by the Lord; we too have been set free. Yet we need to be set free time and time again, for only a free Church is a credible Church. . . .

Peter and Paul bequeath to us the image of a Church entrusted to our hands, yet guided by the Lord with fidelity and tender love, for it is he who guides the Church. A Church that is weak, yet finds strength in the presence of God. The image of a Church set free and capable of offering the world the freedom that the world by itself cannot give: freedom from sin and death, from resignation, and from the sense of injustice and the loss of hope that dehumanizes the lives of the women and men of our time.[76]

Pray

From the Letter of Paul to the Ephesians:

> For this reason I kneel before the Father, from whom every family in heaven and on earth is named, that he may grant you in accord with the riches of his glory to be strengthened with power through his Spirit in the inner self, and that Christ may dwell in your hearts through faith; that you, rooted and grounded in love, may have strength to comprehend with all the holy ones what is the breadth and length and height and depth, and to know the love of Christ that surpasses knowledge, so that you may be filled with all the fullness of God. (3:14-19)

July

THE PRECIOUS BLOOD

As we head into the dog days of summer with no major liturgical celebrations in sight, I'm tempted to ignore the liturgical calendar. July, however, offers a dazzling highlight: we focus on the Precious Blood of Jesus. In the midst of scorching summer days that blur together, a tremendous gift stands out:

God chose to take on a body pulsing with blood.

He spilled his blood.

He gave priests the power to transform mere wine into his blood.

And he did it all for our sake.

We are nourished again and again by this gift and are fed by it every time we attend Mass. How fitting that we should set aside an entire month to pray about and ponder such a mystery.

Pray

Lord, it is so easy to take you for granted. Every week at Mass, we're fed by your Body and your Blood, and it can almost feel routine. Please help me never take for granted the astounding gift you've given us. Your Blood feeds me, sustains me, nourishes me. Thank you, Lord, for the gift of your Precious Blood.

Consider looking up and praying the Litany of the Most Precious Blood of Jesus.

Liturgical Color

Green, for Ordinary Time

A Peek into July's Possibilities

JULY 11
Memorial of St. Benedict

JULY 14
Memorial of St. Kateri Tekakwitha

JULY 15
Memorial of St. Bonaventure

JULY 16
Optional Memorial of Our Lady of Mount Carmel

JULY 22
Feast of St. Mary Magdalene

JULY 28
Optional Memorial of Bl. Stanley Rother

JULY 31
Memorial of St. Ignatius of Loyola

July 11

ST. BENEDICT (C. 480–547)

*Namesake of the Order of St. Benedict (OSB), known as
the father of monasticism in the Western world; patron of
Europe, monks, farmers, engineers, students, and against
kidney and inflammatory disease and poison*

Book two of St. Gregory the Great's *Dialogues* focuses entirely on St. Benedict and consists mostly of miraculous stories about the saint. It's our primary source of information about St. Benedict; other than that, we know very little of this man who has wielded enormous influence on the monastic way of life.

Benedict probably studied in Rome as a teen. But repulsed by the immorality of the city, he fled to solitude, living as a hermit for a few years and immersing himself in contemplative prayer. His holiness and dedication to God attracted others, and a group of monks tried to draft him as their abbot. Benedict was reluctant at first, then agreed, only to find that the men resisted his attempts to institute a firm rule. Their resistance reached murderous levels; it's said they tried to poison him. St. Gregory tells the story of a poisoned cup shattering after Benedict prayed over it.

Future followers of Benedict were more open to his ideas for community, and his influence on monastic life cannot be overstated. He formed at least a dozen monasteries, culminating in the famous monastery at Monte Cassino, which flourished under what would become known as "The Rule of St. Benedict."

We take this rule for granted now, but Benedict's ideas were new at the time. The rule was perceptive and understanding of human nature, while still encouraging complete devotion to God. The spirit of its seventy-three chapters has been summarized as "Pray and work," and Benedict called prayer "the work of God." Benedictines are also known for their charism, or gift, of hospitality.

- "Pray and work" is a motto we can all live by. St. Benedict didn't separate these actions but saw them as part of a whole. When we pray, we are doing the work of God, and when we work, we can offer our actions as a prayer. Is there a part of your job that you dislike? Try offering it as a sacrificial prayer for the sake of someone in need.

He who labors as he prays lifts his heart to God with his hands.

—St. Benedict[77]

July 14

ST. KATERI TEKAKWITHA
(C. 1656–1680)

First indigenous American to be canonized;
patron of ecologists and the environment

Known now as the Lily of the Mohawks, she was originally Tekakwitha ("One who walks groping for her way"). She took the name Kateri (Catherine, from St. Catherine of Siena) when she was baptized.

Tekakwitha's mother, an Algonquin and a Christian, was captured by the Iroquois and given in marriage to the Mohawk chief. When a smallpox epidemic hit, Tekakwitha was orphaned and lost her brother too. The four-year-old was also infected by the virus and left disfigured and partially blind.

Tekakwitha lived under the care of an uncle who became the Mohawk chief. Her uncle wanted nothing to do with the Jesuit missionaries who had arrived, but Tekakwitha, over time, was strangely moved by what she regularly heard from the "Blackrobes."

Though her uncle wanted her to marry, she refused. At the age of nineteen, she sought Baptism, which brought scorn and ridicule from her relatives. Fleeing persecution, she embarked on a two-hundred-mile trip, on foot, to settle in a Christian village near Montreal. Here she prayed, fasted, grew in holiness and knowledge of the faith, shared stories of God with others, and dedicated herself to helping the sick and the elderly.

Kateri attended Mass twice daily, when possible, and had an extraordinary devotion to the Eucharist. She died during Holy Week in 1680, when she was twenty-four years old. In Canada her feast day is April 17.

- Kateri adopted a faith that was strange to many of her family and friends. Have you ever had to defend your faith to a family member or someone else close to you? How did you handle that? Is there anything you wish you had done differently?

Jesus, I love you!

—Traditionally acknowledged to be the
last words of St. Kateri

Pilgrimage Alert

Our Lady of Martyrs Shrine is in the small village of Auriesville in Futonville, New York, the birthplace of St. Kateri. The shrine is dedicated to her and to three Jesuit missionaries who were martyred there. Find out more at ourladyofmartyrsshrine.org. The Cross in the Woods in Indian River, Michigan, also commemorates St. Kateri.

July 15

ST. BONAVENTURE (1221–1274)

Religious, bishop, theologian, mystic, Doctor of the Church;
patron of gastrointestinal and bowel disorders

Bonaventure said that he nearly died of an illness as a child but was cured through the intercession of St. Francis of Assisi. It's not clear when this happened or if St. Francis was present in person, but some years later, the young man, who had been baptized John, became a Franciscan and took the name Bonaventure, which means "good fortune."

Dubbed "The Seraphic Doctor" for his mystical, angelic ("seraphic") writings, Bonaventure was a scholar, theologian, teacher, author, and cardinal. The Franciscans elected him general minister in 1257, a time of deep dissension within the order following St. Francis' death. Because of that role, Bonaventure is often considered the second founder of the Franciscans.

Bonaventure is an example of the melding of many talents and the blending of a contemplative and active faith life. He reminds us that we don't have to choose to be either active or contemplative; we simply need to pay attention to the gifts God has given us and follow the paths God puts before us as we use our talents for his glory.

- Bonaventure wrote about the miraculous cure that St. Francis is said to have brought about in his life. Is it easy or difficult for you to believe in miracles? Have you ever felt you've been in the presence of one?

That heart is free which is held by no love other than God.
—St. Bonaventure[78]

July 16

OUR LADY OF MOUNT CARMEL

Connect

In the twelfth century, a group of hermits living on Mount Carmel in Palestine became known for their devotion to Mary. In the thirteenth century, when the ongoing Crusades in the Holy Land made life on Carmel untenable, these "Brothers of the Blessed Virgin Mary of Mount Carmel" settled in Europe. Known simply as the Carmelites, the men and women of this religious order—whose spirituality has always had close ties to Our Lady—include such spiritual giants as St. Thérèse of Lisieux, St. Teresa of Ávila, and St. John of the Cross. These well-known Carmelite saints have inspired many with their Marian devotion and simple, or "little," ways of growing closer to God.

Tradition tells us that a Carmelite named Simon Stock had an encounter with Mary in which she gave him a scapular (an apron-like garment that goes over the shoulders of the wearer). This brown garment became the habit of the Carmelites; much reduced in size, the scapular has since morphed into a popular devotion for the everyday Catholic. This scapular consists of two pieces of small brown wool connected by strings, allowing the wool pieces to rest on the chest and back. After initial enrollment in this devotion, scapular medals can be worn in place of the fabric version.

Wearers of the scapular promise devotion to Mary and holy living. They in turn take solace in being "clothed" in Mary's protection.

To Ponder or Do

- The wearing of a scapular, whether the wool one or a medal, is a constant reminder of the holiness of the Blessed Mother and our call to holiness too. If you wear a scapular, consider reviewing your enrollment or renewing your promises to the Lord through this devotion. If you've never worn one, you might read up on it and pray about it. Are you called to have this regular reminder of Our Lady at your fingertips?

- If you have kids, talk with them about Our Lady of Mount Carmel. Throw in a treat—something caramel, of course! Voila: feast day complete.

- Consider these words of St. Thérèse of Lisieux: "Pray especially to Our Blessed Mother Mary, placing all your intentions into her hands."[79]

Pray

Lord, you give us so many ways to remember and turn to you: through sacramentals, such as scapulars and medals; through the example of a rich variety of religious orders and their myriad gifts and charisms; and through the example of Our Lady, our mother and advocate. Thank you for the rich tapestry that is the Church.

July 22

ST. MARY MAGDALENE
(FIRST CENTURY)

Follower of Christ, the first to see Christ after the resurrection; patron of converts, women, contemplatives

We don't know a lot about Mary, but we do know she was a special disciple of Jesus. Current Biblical scholarship finds no evidence that she was a prostitute or that she was the woman of Luke 7:37-38, who wept as she anointed Jesus' feet. Scripture tells us only that Jesus drove seven demons from her (see 8:2), that she saw Jesus crucified (see John 19:25), that she was the first to have the privilege of seeing the risen Jesus and the first to bring the good news to the apostles (see 20:1-2).

Mary's fierce and tender love for Jesus, as well as her courage and devotion, leap from the pages of Scripture and draw us to this model disciple, who never gave up on the Lord and knew he would never give up on her. A brief roundup of Bible verses that specifically mention her: Matthew 27:56, 61; 28:1-10; Mark 15:40, 47; 16:1-11; Luke 8:2; 24:10; John 19:25; 20:1-18.

- Ask St. Mary Magdalene to pray for you today, that you may have her bold faith, fearless love, and never-ending gratitude.

The Magdalene, most of all, is the model I like to follow. That boldness of hers, which would be so amazing if it weren't the boldness of a lover, won the heart of Jesus, and how it fascinates mine!

— St. Thérèse of Lisieux[80]

July 28

BL. STANLEY ROTHER
(1935–1981)

Priest, martyr

Stanley Rother, a farmer turned priest from Okarche, Oklahoma, seems an unlikely candidate for martyrdom in Guatemala, but that's where his vocation took him. He barely made it through the seminary; he was asked to leave at one point because of poor grades. Nevertheless, his bishop, recognizing Rother's potential, encouraged him to pursue the priesthood. Stanley went on to attend Mount St. Mary's Seminary in Maryland.

Stanley was ordained for the diocese of Oklahoma/Tulsa in 1963, and he served five years in his home diocese before requesting permission to join the diocese's mission in Santiago Atitlán, Guatemala, serving the indigenous Tz'utujil people. Over the course of thirteen years, Fr. Rother became a beloved figure there, offering multiple daily Masses, performing hundreds of Baptisms each year, working side by side in the fields with his parishioners, starting a farmers' co-op and a clinic, helping translate the New Testament into the Tz'utujil language, and preaching in Tz'utujil as well. His work with the native language was all the more remarkable given that his failure to grasp Latin lay behind many of his struggles during his seminary years.

As Guatemala's civil war edged closer to their rural area, parishioners began to be abducted and murdered. Fr. Stanley witnessed assassinations, including that of the deacon of his parish. He returned to Oklahoma for a visit in 1981, returning to Guatemala in time to celebrate Holy Week and Easter with his people. He knew his name was on a death list. He wrote in his last letter home,

> The reality is that we are in danger. But we don't know when or what form the government will use to further repress the Church. . . . Given the situation, I am not ready to leave here just yet. . . . But if it is my destiny that I should give my life here, then so be it.[81]

On July 28, 1981, at 1:30 a.m., three masked men broke into the rectory, beat Fr. Rother, and shot him in the head. Other wounds indicated he'd been tortured, but he hadn't cried out, presumably to save the lives of nine nuns who were in a convent nearby and other people who were staying at the rectory.

Pope Francis declared Fr. Rother a martyr for the faith on December 1, 2016, making him the first martyr of the United States and the first priest born in the United States to be beatified.

- Fr. Rother's devotion to his flock and his courage in remaining with them are beyond inspiring. Have you ever been in a situation in which it felt dangerous to proclaim or share your faith? Ask Fr. Rother today to help you always be "a sign of love."

The shepherd cannot run at the first sign of danger. Pray for us that we may be a sign of the love of Christ for our people, that our presence among them will fortify them to endure these sufferings in preparation for the coming of the Kingdom.

—Bl. Stanley Rother [82]

PILGRIMAGE ALERT

Holy Trinity Catholic Church, in Okarche, Oklahoma, was Fr. Rother's parish as a child. He was buried in Resurrection Memorial Cemetery in Oklahoma City, but his heart is enshrined in Santiago Atitlán, Guatemala. Visit archokc.org/shrine for more information.

July 31

ST. IGNATIUS OF LOYOLA
(1491–1556)

Priest, mystic, founder of the Society of Jesus (Jesuits);
patron of the Society of Jesus, soldiers, educators

A cannonball shatters the legs of a military man. During his long and painful convalescence, he has little to do but read books. When his first choice—juicy tales of chivalry and romance—is not available, he takes what he can get: a book about the life of Christ and a book about saints. The former soldier finds the material surprisingly absorbing, and his life is transformed.

Does this sound likely? It's the true story of St. Ignatius, who would go on to lay the groundwork for the Society of Jesus and develop his set of spiritual exercises, which are still used by religious and laity the world over.

The transformation didn't happen overnight; most conversions don't. Ignatius embarked on a lengthy spiritual trek that eventually led him to the priesthood and the founding, with early followers, of the Society of Jesus. On the way—in fact, at the very start—Ignatius began to record his feelings as he read and meditated on Scripture. His reflections—about such things as gratitude, God's unconditional love, Jesus' suffering and death, consolation and desolation, the joy of the Christian life—eventually became his *Spiritual Exercises*. Originally a handbook for a thirty-day retreat, the Exercises continue to have a profound impact on the faith lives of millions.

The Lord used Ignatius' interest in juicy tales to draw him into a dramatic new way of being. What a powerful illustration of how, with God, our "winding roads shall be made straight" (Luke 3:5).

The motto of the Jesuits is straightforward: *Ad Majorem Dei Gloriam*, "for the greater glory of God." Ignatius' beautiful prayer, *Suscipe* (Receive), below, captures his intense love for God and humble abandonment to God's will.

- The lives of the saints inspired Ignatius to seek God with all his heart. Their stories spurred him on to sainthood and transformed him into a light that has illuminated countless other lives. What saint has most inspired you? How do you like to honor that saint?

Suscipe

Take, Lord, and receive all my liberty,
my memory, my understanding,
and my entire will,
All I have and call my own.

You have given all to me.
To you, Lord, I return it.

Everything is yours; do with it what you will.
Give me only your love and your grace,
that is enough for me.

—St. Ignatius of Loyola[83]

August

THE ASSUMPTION OF THE BLESSED VIRGIN MARY

In August we meet rich and varied saints, from St. Teresa Benedicta of the Cross to St. Monica and her wayward son turned Church Doctor, St. Augustine. This month also offers another chance to focus on the unique role Mary plays in salvation history, as we observe the Assumption of the Blessed Virgin Mary on August 15 and the Queenship of Mary on August 22. These feasts are reminders of the corporeal reality of heaven.

It's easy to "spiritualize" heaven, imagining transcendent music and ethereal beings enjoying eternal bliss. But our faith teaches us that, like Mary, we will have bodies in heaven. While it's hard to fully grasp what that will look and feel like, this month simply embrace the truth of bodily resurrection, knowing that God has our backs on the details.

Pray

Mary, pray for me, that my zeal to be where you are—fully present with the Lord, body and soul, adoring him for all eternity—will never wane.

Liturgical Color

Green, for Ordinary Time

A Peek into August's Possibilities

AUGUST 6
Feast of the Transfiguration of the Lord

AUGUST 9
Optional Memorial of St. Teresa Benedicta of the Cross (St. Edith Stein)

AUGUST 12
Optional Memorial of St. Jane Frances de Chantal

AUGUST 14
Memorial of St. Maximilian Mary Kolbe

AUGUST 15
Solemnity of the Assumption of the Blessed Virgin Mary

AUGUST 27
Memorial of St. Monica

AUGUST 28
Memorial of St. Augustine

August 6

FEAST OF THE TRANSFIGURATION OF THE LORD

Connect

In the moment of the Transfiguration—a moment so important that it's found in three of the four Gospels—Peter, James, and John, who are fearful because of Jesus' prediction of his passion, have the opportunity to see Jesus in a completely new way. As Pope Francis said in his Angelus address on February 28, 2021,

> The Gospel says: He "led them up a high mountain" [Mark 9:2]. In the Bible, the mountain always has a special significance: it is the elevated place where heaven and earth touch each other, where Moses and the prophets had the extraordinary experience of encountering God. Climbing the mountain is drawing somewhat close to God. Jesus climbs up with the three disciples and they stop at the top of the mountain. Here, he is transfigured before them. His face radiant and his garments

glistening, which provide a preview of the image as the Risen One, offer to those frightened men *the light,* the light of hope, the light *to pass through the shadows:* death will not be the end of everything, because it will open to the glory of the Resurrection. Thus, Jesus announces his death; he takes them up the mountain and shows them what will happen afterwards, the Resurrection.

As the Apostle Peter exclaimed (cf. v. 5), it is good to pause with the Lord on the mountain, to live this "preview" of light. . . . It is a call to remember, especially when we go through a difficult trial—and many of you know what it means to go through a difficult trial—that the Lord is Risen and does not allow darkness to have the last word.[84]

In witnessing the Transfiguration of Jesus, Peter, James, and John were spiritually transformed. Though they would still stumble, they knew that darkness would not have the last word.

To Ponder or Do

- Read the three accounts of the Transfiguration in Matthew 17:1-8, Mark 9:2-8, and Luke 9:28-36.

- Consider how Peter, James, and John must have felt when they witnessed the Transfiguration of Jesus. They were suddenly in the presence of Jesus' full and divine glory. It must have been overpowering. Can you imagine such a feeling?

  Think about the times you have most powerfully felt God's presence. If you keep a journal, spend a little time writing about those moments. Did you set aside time to make those moments happen, or did they come to you out of the blue?

- Think about a time when you feared that darkness would "have the last word." What helped you climb the mountain and see the illuminating light of Jesus in a new way?

Pray

Lord, when I feel fear and uncertainty about the future, give me, as Pope Francis said, "the light of hope, the light to pass through the shadows" and the firm knowledge that "death will not be the end of everything, because it will open to the glory of the Resurrection."

August 9

ST. TERESA BENEDICTA OF THE CROSS (ST. EDITH STEIN) (1891–1942)

Philosopher, religious, martyr; patron of Europe

Edith Stein, a brilliant young woman, decided by the age of fourteen that God did not exist. The youngest of eleven children in a Polish Jewish family, she entered university, studied philosophy, pursued doctoral studies, and fought for a position as a professor, which she was denied because she was a woman. She was later denied another position because she was Jewish, but she persisted in her studies, her writing, and her quest for truth.

In 1921, while staying with friends, Edith pulled the autobiography of St. Teresa of Ávila from their bookcase and spent the entire night reading it. Later she wrote, "When I had finished the book, I said to myself: This is the truth."[85]

Edith was baptized several months later. Immediately she wanted to join the Carmelite order, but her spiritual directors advised her to wait. She taught, spoke on women's issues, translated works of John Henry Newman and Thomas Aquinas, and followed other academic pursuits. She saw scholarship as an authentic and valuable way to serve God.

In 1933 Edith joined the Carmelite Convent of Cologne and took the name St. Teresa Benedicta of the Cross. When she made her final profession of vows in 1938, she adopted the words of St. John of the Cross: "Henceforth my only vocation is to love."[86] Her last academic work, "The Science of the Cross," was on St. John and suffering.

As Nazi hatred and anti-Semitism spread, the convent's prioress did her best to protect Edith, secretly taking her across the border into the Netherlands to the presumed safety of the Carmelite Convent in Echt. There Edith's sister Rosa, also a convert, served as a lay sister. Germany invaded the Netherlands in May 1940 and in 1942 began deporting the country's

Jews. The Dutch bishops denounced this policy. In retaliation, the Nazis hunted down Jewish converts to Catholicism.

The two sisters were arrested on August 2, 1942. According to witnesses, Edith said to Rosa as they were led away, "Come, let us go for our people."[87] They were briefly held at Westerbork, a transit center, where a fellow prisoner said of St. Teresa that "she walked among the prisoners, talking and praying like a saint. She spoke in such a humble and clear way. . . . A talk with her was like a voyage into another world."[88]

St. Teresa Benedicta of the Cross and her sister Rosa were murdered in a gas chamber at Auschwitz on August 9, 1942. At her beatification on May 1, 1987, Pope John Paul II said,

> We bow down before the testimony of the life and death of Edith Stein, an outstanding daughter of Israel and at the same time a daughter of the Carmelite Order, Sister Teresa Benedicta of the Cross, a personality who united within her rich life a dramatic synthesis of our century. It was the synthesis of a history full of deep wounds that are still hurting . . . and also the synthesis of the full truth about man. All this came together in a single heart that remained restless and unfulfilled until it finally found rest in God.[89]

- St. Teresa shows us what it means to search for truth and be willing to set aside everything we've known to follow God into that truth. Have you ever discovered a truth of the faith that shook you or challenged you?

My longing for truth was a single prayer.
—St. Teresa Benedicta of the Cross[90]

August 12

ST. JANE FRANCES DE CHANTAL
(1572–1641)

*Wife, mother, religious, founder of a religious community;
patron of widows, wives, mothers*

After seven years of marriage and several children, Jane de Chantal's husband was killed in a hunting accident. Devastated—their marriage was intensely happy—Jane moved in with her mean-tempered, demanding father-in-law, who threatened otherwise to disinherit her children. She spent eight years at his castle raising her children and her husband's illegitimate daughter, caring for the children of her father-in-law's difficult and demanding mistress, and visiting the sick. She took a vow of chastity.

Jane fell under the spiritual direction of an unsympathetic priest, who made her promise never to consult anyone else for spiritual advice. She later described these years as purgatory, but her faith sustained her. As she prayed her way through the challenges, Jane had a vision of an unknown priest. He, she understood, would become her spiritual director.

Soon she met St. Francis de Sales, then bishop of Geneva, and recognized him as the priest of her vision. Thus began one of the most famous spiritual friendships in history. Together they started the Congregation of the Visitation for women who were considered too old or too frail to find a place in other religious communities. To those who criticized her for accepting such candidates, she said, "What do you want me to do? I like sick people myself; I'm on their side."[91]

Jane met St. Vincent de Paul when she was in Paris opening a convent. He later said of her,

> She was full of faith, yet all her life had been tormented by thoughts against it. While apparently enjoying the peace and easiness of mind of souls who have reached a high state of virtue, she suffered such interior trials that she often told me her mind was so filled with all sorts of temptations and abominations that she had to strive not to look within herself. . . . But for all that suffering her face never lost its serenity, nor did she once relax in the fidelity God asked of her. And so I regard her as one of the holiest souls I have ever met on this earth.[92]

Always enormously encouraging to others, Jane never gave up her trust in the Lord in spite of her many spiritual trials. We can turn confidently to this saint for her intercession; she knows what it's like to be a wife and mother, to have her life turned upside down, to experience loss, and to carry on in one's vocation in spite of ongoing challenges. She also knows a thing or two about spiritual friendship and its immeasurable value.

- St. Jane shows us honesty, forthrightness, and a willingness to challenge the status quo when necessary. She also models the power of spiritual friendship. Do you have a spiritual friend, someone you can be completely honest with about your spiritual highs and lows?

If we patiently accept through love all that God allows to happen, then we will begin to taste even here on earth something of the delights the saints experience in heaven.

—St. Jane Frances de Chantal[93]

August 14

ST. MAXIMILIAN MARY KOLBE
(1894–1941)

Priest, martyr, founder of the Militia of the Immaculata and publisher of Knight of the Immaculata *magazine; patron of drug addicts, prisoners, political prisoners, families, journalists. Pope John Paul II named him the "patron saint for our difficult [twentieth] century."*[94]

When he was in his early teens, Maximilian Kolbe wondered, as many teens do, what his future held. He already had a strong devotion to Mary, so he asked her in prayer to guide him. One night the Blessed Mother appeared to him and offered him one of two crowns: a white crown, which represented purity, and a red crown, which signified martyrdom. He accepted both.

Maximilian went on to become a Franciscan priest, earn doctorates in philosophy and theology, and teach at a seminary. His devotion to Mary led him to found a movement he called the Militia of the Immaculata, to promote devotion to the Blessed Mother. His drive to evangelize overrode any limitations. In spite of financial and health issues, Maximilian established a mission in Japan, a publishing house, and a radio station. He often said that the greatest spiritual poison of our time is indifference, and he deflected all praise for any success to Mary.

Critical of the Nazis, Kolbe was arrested in 1939, along with some of his fellow Franciscan friars, then released. Refusing to be silenced—and already sheltering Jews in the monastery—he was arrested again in 1941 and sent to Auschwitz. There he furtively ministered to other prisoners, hearing confessions and encouraging others to forgive their tormentors. Though he was beaten and tortured, he responded with gentleness to everyone. As a fellow prisoner later said, "He was a priest every inch of his burned-out body."[95]

Just a few months after Kolbe arrived at Auschwitz, a prisoner escaped. As a warning to remaining prisoners, the guards chose ten men at random to die by starvation, locked together in a bunker. Francis Gajowniczek, one of those selected, cried out, "My wife! My children!" His plea prompted Kolbe to step forward and volunteer to take his place. In the bunker, Kolbe comforted and spiritually strengthened the men, praying, singing hymns, and reassuring them of his love and the love of God.

After two weeks, only Maximilian was still alive. He was conscious when the guards entered the cell for the last time, and he calmly lifted his arm for their injection of carbolic acid. He was murdered on August 14, the eve of the Solemnity of the Assumption of the Blessed Virgin Mary.

Francis Gajowniczek, for whom Maximilian Kolbe sacrificed his life, attended Kolbe's canonization in 1982.

- Maximilian Kolbe modeled the love of Christ when he gave his life for another man. Consider how you will respond when the Lord asks you to counter hatred with love, no matter how small the incident. When it's hard to follow through, call on St. Maximilian to pray for you.

Hatred is not a creative force: only love is creative.
—St. Maximilian Kolbe[96]

August 15

SOLEMNITY OF THE ASSUMPTION OF THE BLESSED VIRGIN MARY

Connect

People sometimes struggle with Marian doctrines. They can seem so *random*. For example, Pope Pius XII proclaimed the dogma that Mary had been assumed bodily into heaven only in 1950.

But there was really nothing new about this proclamation; it was a formal declaration of a centuries-old belief. There's evidence that theologians and Church leaders discussed the assumption of Mary as early as the sixth century. And by the thirteenth century, there was near-universal agreement about the belief.

It simply made sense: since Mary was born without original sin, she didn't experience all the consequences of original sin, including the kind of death and decomposition of the body that we will experience. The pope's infallible statement in 1950 came, at last, after cardinals, bishops, tens of thousands of priests and religious, and millions of laypeople petitioned the pope to "make it official."

The doctrine of the assumption affirms that Mary received immediately the gift that all faithful believers will eventually experience: body and soul together in heaven, with the Lord for all eternity. And so we celebrate that Mary is in heaven, in possession of her body, not having to wait for the last judgment.

It seems right and fitting. In fact, it would seem *unjust* if Mary had to go through everything we'll have to go through. Let's take comfort in the mental image of Mary, fully present in heaven, praying for us and whisking every petition off to her son.

- Does the assumption of Mary feel unreal to you, or have you always felt comfortable with the doctrine? If it feels strange or unreal, does it help to consider that Mary is already fully in God's presence, as we all hope to be one day?

To Ponder or Do

- Celebrate Mary at Mass. Today is a solemnity and a holy day of obligation. Another word for "obligation" is "engagement." Think of this celebration as a chance to engage with the Lord and his mother.

- Take a few minutes to read the Apostolic Constitution of Pope Pius XII *Munificentissimus Deus*, defining the dogma of the assumption, available at vatican.va. Regarding the clamor for official declaration of the dogma, Pius XII noted that

not only individual Catholics, but also those who could speak for nations or ecclesiastical provinces, and even a considerable number of the Fathers of the [First] Vatican Council, urgently petitioned the Apostolic See to this effect.

During the course of time such postulations and petitions did not decrease but rather grew continually in number and in urgency. In this cause there were pious crusades of prayer. [97]

- In various cultures around the world, this day is celebrated with flowers and with blessings of meals of grapes, wheat, and herbs such as sweet basil. One ancient tradition held that after the fall of Adam and Eve, flowers and herbs lost their fragrance and power, but on the day of Mary's assumption into heaven, all flora regained its sweet scent, and herbs had their healing power returned to them. Celebrate Mary's assumption with a fragrant bouquet of flowers today.

Pray

Hail, Holy Queen, Mother of Mercy,
our life, our sweetness, and our hope.
To thee do we cry,
poor banished children of Eve.
To thee do we send up our sighs,
mourning and weeping in this valley of tears.
Turn then, most gracious advocate,
thine eyes of mercy toward us,
and after this our exile,
show unto us the blessed fruit of thy womb, Jesus.
O clement, O loving,
O sweet Virgin Mary.
Pray for us, O holy Mother of God,
that we may be made worthy of the promises of Christ.

August 27

ST. MONICA (330–387)

Wife, mother; patron of wives, mothers, and conversion

St. Monica, the mother of St. Augustine, is the quintessential model of intercessory prayer for the conversion of others. She was the wife of a pagan man, Patricius, who was critical and unfaithful and did nothing when his mother, who lived with the family, treated Monica with harshness and disrespect. Monica steadfastly prayed for her husband and mother-in-law, and Patricius was baptized just a year before his death in 371. His mother also converted. Monica's faithful example and her heartfelt prayers prevailed.

Monica and Patricius had three children, but of course we know the most about Augustine. He was a wayward soul when he was young, and Monica persisted in various tactics to draw him to Christianity. At one point, she thought that forbidding him to stay at her house or share meals with her would impress upon him the direness of his spiritual circumstances, but after receiving assurance through a vision that Augustine would come back to the faith, she changed her approach and stayed close to her son.

Augustine, however, literally fled his mother's influence. He moved to Rome with his mistress and their child, and then he went on to Milan—with Monica on his trail. In Milan, St. Ambrose became a spiritual director to both Augustine and Monica. St. Ambrose baptized Augustine in 387, and Monica died a short time later. Most of what we know about Monica comes from her son's famous work *Confessions*.

- Monica refused to give up on her beloved child. Though she grieved, worried, and mourned, she also returned repeatedly to prayer. She believed her son would one day embrace the truth. As Augustine himself would so memorably write, "You have made us for yourself, and our hearts are restless until they rest in you."[98]

Is there someone you worry about and pray for? Ask St. Monica to pray. She knows how those tears feel.

[A]nd out of the blood of my mother's heart, through the tears that she poured out by day and by night, was a sacrifice offered unto you for me; and by marvelous ways did you deal with me.

—St. Augustine[99]

August 28

ST. AUGUSTINE (354–430)

Bishop, Doctor of the Church; patron of brewers, theologians, printers

Late have I loved you, beauty so old and so new: late have I loved you.[100]

St. Augustine's conversion unfolded slowly, over years. It was the result of his own intellectual and spiritual inquiry; the influence and prayers of those around him, including his mother; and, of course, God's grace. At one point in his conversion odyssey, he felt strongly drawn to the truth but struggled with the Church's call to chastity. In the *Confessions,* he admitted that he prayed, "Lord, make me chaste, but *not yet.*"

One day, as Augustine struggled mightily with his longing to become a Christian but his inability to move forward, he fled into a garden. There he heard a child playing and chanting, "Take it and read, take it and read." Interpreting this as a sign from the Lord, Augustine flipped the Bible open and landed at Romans 13:13-14: "Let us conduct ourselves becomingly as in the day, not in reveling and drunkenness, not in debauchery and licentiousness, not in quarreling and jealousy. But put on the Lord Jesus Christ, and make no provision for the flesh, to gratify its desires" [RSVCE].[101]

It was a turning point. Both Augustine and his son (who died shortly after this) were baptized. Augustine became a priest in 391 and went on to become one of the greatest theologians in history.

Augustine's dramatic conversion serves as a study of the human condition: we are torn between our worldly wants and the divine embrace. In the end, nothing can satisfy us as God does.

- Do you have regrets about your faith life, or have you always had the gift of belief? Wherever you fall on the spectrum of ongoing conversion, pray today for all souls who struggle with belief and have trouble making the leap of faith.

Late have I loved you, beauty so old and so new: late have I loved you. And see, you were within and I was in the external world and sought you there, and in my unlovely state I plunged into those lovely created things which you made. You were with me, and I was not with you. The lovely things kept me far from you, though if they did not have their existence in you, they had no existence at all. You called and cried out loud and shattered my deafness. You were radiant and resplendent, you put to flight my blindness. You were fragrant, and I drew in my breath and now pant after you. I tasted you, and I feel but hunger and thirst for you. You touched me, and I am set on fire to attain the peace which is yours.

—St. Augustine, *The Confessions*[102]

September

THE HOLY CROSS

Leaves curl at autumn's imminent arrival, and the liturgical year moves steadily forward, ushering us through Ordinary Time. But again, nothing about ordered time is monotonous or dull. September offers dramatic feasts: the Birth of the Blessed Virgin Mary, the Exaltation of the Holy Cross, the Archangels Michael, Gabriel, and Raphael. The grandeur of God's vision and the richness of his plans shine forth this month with a gleam as golden and glowing as the sun on a crisp fall day.

Pray

Lord, it's easy for me to take the cross for granted. I'm aware of its meaning every day, but sometimes I don't truly *see* it or embrace what the cross really is. It is a visual representation of your radical and complete love for me. You suffered on the cross for *me*. What am I to do with that knowledge? Help me always remember your complete, all-encompassing love.

Liturgical Color

Green, for Ordinary Time

A Peek into September's Possibilities

SEPTEMBER 3
Memorial of Pope St. Gregory the Great

SEPTEMBER 5
Optional Memorial of St. Teresa of Kolkata

SEPTEMBER 8
Feast of the Birth of the Blessed Virgin Mary

SEPTEMBER 14
Feast of the Exaltation of the Holy Cross

SEPTEMBER 17
Optional Memorial of St. Hildegard of Bingen

SEPTEMBER 21
Feast of St. Matthew the Evangelist

SEPTEMBER 29
Feast of Sts. Michael, Gabriel, and Raphael, Archangels

SEPTEMBER 30
Memorial of St. Jerome

September 3

POPE ST. GREGORY THE GREAT
(C. 540-604)

Priest, bishop, pope, Doctor of the Church;
patron of teachers, musicians, singers

You've heard the pope referred to as the "servant of the servants of God," and we can thank St. Gregory for that beautiful designation. Gregory was truly a servant. He served as the prefect of Rome for a time, but when his father died, he stepped away from public office and began a new "career": founder of monasteries—seven in all—including one in his own home. He wanted only to love and serve God as a monk.

Ordained in 578, Gregory was elected pope just twelve years later. It was an office he didn't want to hold, preferring the monastic life. Nevertheless, he continued in "servant mode" and did what he had to do. His energy seemed to know no bounds.

Gregory set about reforming the Church and its liturgy, and his effect was profound. He is credited with Gregorian chant. He reformed the clergy and spent endless amounts of money in ways that Jesus would approve: for the poor, needy, and sick. His extensive writings and his shaping of the papacy had ongoing influence in the Church and earned him the titles of Doctor of the Church and "the Great."

- St. Gregory wanted a quiet, monastic life but instead ended up carrying the largest earthly burden a Catholic can carry: being the servant of the servants of God. In that role, he was "riveted together" with his fellow Christians. Is there an area of your life in which you've decided what you want but God seems to be calling you to something else?

When we are linked up by the power of prayer, we, as it were, hold each other's hand as we walk side by side along a slippery path; and thus by the bounteous disposition of charity, it comes about that the harder each one leans on the other, the more firmly we are riveted together in brotherly love.

—St. Gregory the Great[103]

September 5

ST. TERESA OF KOLKATA
(1910–1997)

Religious, founder of the Missionaries of Charity;
patron of World Youth Day

Agnes Gonxha Bojaxhiu, a young Catholic woman from Skopje, North Macedonia, followed a calling to religious life and became known the world over as Mother Teresa and now St. Teresa of Kolkata. Her face is iconic, her diminutive stature well-known, and her devotion and service to suffering human beings—"the poorest of the poor"—inspiring by any measure of the word.

It's easy to place this tiny woman on a pedestal and presume she embraced her vocation and never looked back, but we know better. No one's life travels in a straight or perfect line, and Agnes' life was no different. She originally joined the Sisters of Loreto and taught school in India. But one day, during a train ride to Darjeeling, she had an encounter with the Lord that she afterward referred to as "a call within a call."[104]

In some divine and intimate way, Jesus communicated his thirst for souls to Sr. Teresa. He asked her to leave the Loreto order and begin something new: an order dedicated to the poorest of the poor. She would serve those who were suffering the most, and even live among them.

Mother Teresa began her work by receiving nursing training and opening a school for children who lived in the slums. Her simple white sari with three blue stripes would become the habit of the Missionaries of Charity, recognized around the world. Her order now serves the poor and suffering in more than 130 countries.

Several years after her death in 1997, some of St. Teresa's letters revealed that for fifty years—almost from the moment she began her new ministry until her death—she endured extreme spiritual dryness, even darkness, and a sense of the absence of God. The darkness lifted only once, briefly. In this, as well as in her selfless service to the poor, Teresa displayed the ultimate in faithfulness: she united her suffering with the suffering of Jesus on the cross and continued to serve as he'd called her to serve. She shows us that God can always write straight with the crooked lines of our lives, whether we feel him at work in us or not.

- St. Teresa started her mission by simply getting to know her neighbors and finding out what they needed. Her worldwide work did not begin as an ambitious "mission." She simply began with one person, and she kept going. Who is the one person closest to you whom God is asking you to love or serve?

I never look at the masses as my responsibility. I can only love one person at a time. I can feed only one person at a time. Just one, one, one. You get closer to Christ by coming closer to each other.

—St. Teresa of Kolkata[105]

September 8

FEAST OF THE BIRTH OF THE BLESSED VIRGIN MARY

Connect

Typically the Church observes the day of a saint's death as a feast day because on that date, the saint entered into the glory of heaven. But the Church celebrates the day of Mary's birth because, as Pope Paul VI wrote in his Apostolic Exhortation *Marialis Cultus*, Mary's birth represents "the hope of the entire world and the dawn of salvation."[106]

We don't know the exact day that Mary was born, but the Church helps by fixing events in time and space for us. December 8 is the day we celebrate Mary's immaculate conception, and nine months later, Mother Church reminds us to celebrate the day of her birth.

When I was newly Catholic, I accepted Marian practices, devotions, and doctrines only because I had already accepted the teaching authority of the magisterium. I may not have fully understood every nuance of the assumption of Mary or exactly how and why the Rosary had developed as it did, but I put these things in a mental file I called "The Church knows better than I do." Then I went about living my new Catholic life.

In accepting these teachings, I noticed something happening. I found myself turning to Mary more. I thought about her more often, and I discovered that I could relate to events in her life. She became, in my mind and heart, a real person, a woman who was born, lived a complicated life of service and obedience to God, and was now in heaven, rooting for me.

Mary became someone whose birthday I wanted to celebrate because she was, in short, not only the mother of Jesus but the mother of all of us. My mother. She is a woman, daughter, wife, mother, friend, role model, and intercessor extraordinaire.

To Ponder or Do

- Add Mary's birthday to your calendar. Every year, say a prayer on her birthday, thanking God for Mary's role in our salvation and for her fiat, her yes. Spend a little time with these words from Pope Francis:

  [W]e can look to Our Lady, small, holy, without sin, pure, chosen to become the mother of God. . . . How do I journey in my story? Do I let God walk with me? Do I let him walk with me or do I want to walk alone? Do I let him caress me, help me, forgive me, lead me forward to reach the encounter with Jesus Christ?[107]

- Search online for "The Protoevangelium of James" and the Catholic Encyclopedia to find apocryphal stories about Mary and her parents, Joachim and

Anne. Although these writings are not part of Scripture, they offer insight into some of the Church's shaping of Marian doctrine and, in this case, the birth of Mary.

- Celebrate! It's a simple observance and may not seem grand enough for the Queen of Heaven and earth, but have a special meal, a glass of wine, or a sweet treat. Let your heavenly mother know you're thinking of her.

Pray

Lord, thank you for the wisdom and beauty of your plan for Mary. Thank you for reminders within the liturgical calendar of the things we take for granted: the conception of Mary, the birth of this extraordinary woman, her acceptance of your claim on her life, and the devotion with which she lived, offering everything to you. Thank you too for Mother Church, who guides us day by day, month by month, and year by year, reminding us to take the time to observe, reflect, and celebrate.

September 14

FEAST OF THE EXALTATION OF THE HOLY CROSS

Connect

If you've ever prayed the Stations of the Cross, you've said, "We adore you, O Christ, and we praise you. Because by your holy cross, you have redeemed the world." We associate this prayer with praying the stations during Lent, but today the liturgical calendar gives us further opportunity to focus on the glory of the cross.

As Pope Benedict XVI wrote,

> The Cross itself has become God's glorification, the glory of God made manifest in the love of the Son. This glory extends beyond the moment into the whole sweep of history. This glory is life. It is on the Cross that we see it, hidden yet powerful: the glory of God, the transformation of death into life.[108]

By instituting this feast—it goes back to at least the early fourth century—it's as if the Church is saying, "So what if it's September and you had no plans to pray the stations? Take a few minutes out of your day to exalt the cross."

To Ponder or Do

- Spend some time with these words from St. Andrew of Crete:

> If you would understand that the cross is Christ's triumph, hear what he himself also said: "When I am lifted up, then I will draw all men to myself." Now you can see that the cross is Christ's glory and triumph.[109]

Jesus Christ allowed himself to be crucified, and his choice defeated death forever. We are the blessed recipients of God's triumphant plan. How often do we thank him for enduring the cross on our behalf?

- This feast has been celebrated for hundreds of years. According to tradition, it grew out of St. Helena's finding of the true cross. Search online using the terms "St. Helena," "Constantine," and "the Cross" to find more about the institution of this feast.

- Do you wear a cross around your neck? It may seem strange that we wear what was once a symbol of punishment and torture, but when we take to heart St. Andrew's words, we're reminded that the cross is a sign of triumph. When we wear this symbol, we wear a reminder of Christ's saving work. If you don't wear a cross, consider adopting this devotional reminder.

- The next time you make the Sign of the Cross, take a moment to really think about what Jesus did. Slow down as you say the words "In the name of the Father, and of the Son, and of the Holy Spirit," and let your "Amen" be a heartfelt proclamation.

Pray

Pray the words that St. Francis prayed before the crucifix of San Damiano:

Most High glorious God,
enlighten the darkness of my heart.
Grant me an upright faith,
secure hope and perfect charity.
Fill me with understanding and knowledge
that I may fulfill your command. Amen.[110]

September 17

ST. HILDEGARD OF BINGEN
(1098–1179)

Writer, poet, composer, mystic, theologian, abbess,
Doctor of the Church

Born to nobility, Hildegard experienced visions of the Lord from the time she was three years old. It was clear that she was destined for greatness far beyond earthly wealth.

Because she was ailing and frail, her parents entrusted Hildegard's care to a Benedictine abbess, Blessed Jutta, who raised her from age eight to eighteen. Then Hildegard became a nun in Jutta's monastery. Jutta recognized and nurtured Hildegard's natural, or perhaps divinely infused, knowledge of the faith, as well as her innate understanding of music, science, healing herbs, and medicine. When Jutta died in 1136, Hildegard, who was known for her holiness and was beloved by all, was named abbess.

At the request of her spiritual director, Hildegard recorded some of the visions she'd had since childhood, in her book *Scivias* [*Know the Ways*]. Her major works of theology include as well *The Book of the Merits of Life* and *The Book of Divine Works*. In an age when few women wrote, she also composed hymns, poems, nearly four hundred letters that remain extant, and treatises on botany and medicine.

Though her works were approved by her bishop and by Pope Eugenius III, and though popes and kings often consulted her, Hildegard sometimes found herself in trouble. For example, she permitted the burial of a young noble who had been excommunicated, insisting that he had repented and received the sacraments before his death and therefore deserved a Christian burial. Church authorities disagreed and issued an interdict, a censure that halted the celebration of Mass and the sacraments at her monastery. Hildegard obeyed the interdict—it was lifted only shortly before her death—but maintained that her position was the correct one.

Hildegard died on September 17, 1179. Pope Benedict XVI canonized her in 2012 and, soon after, declared her a Doctor of the Church—one of only four women to have the title. The pope said of her,

> Hildegard asks herself and us the fundamental question, whether it is possible to know God: This is theology's principal task. Her answer is completely positive: through faith, as through a door, the human person is able to approach this knowledge. [111]

- Hildegard's gifts may seem far out of reach to most of us, but Pope Benedict XVI reminds us that she is relatable in that she asks the fundamental question: "Can we know God?" Hildegard said yes. How would you respond to that question?

Man, too, is God's handiwork, like every other creature. But man is also God's journeyman and the foreshadowing of the mysteries of God.

—St. Hildegard of Bingen[112]

September 21

ST. MATTHEW, EVANGELIST, APOSTLE

Connect

Wealthy and hated: as a tax collector, that was Matthew's position in society. We may not be wealthy, or hated, or have a universally despised profession, so where and how do we connect with Matthew? Take a look at the call of Matthew, found in Matthew 9:9-13:

> As Jesus passed on from there, he saw a man named Matthew sitting at the customs post. He said to him, "Follow me." And he got up and followed him. While he was at table in his house, many tax collectors and sinners came and sat with Jesus and his disciples. The Pharisees saw this and said to his disciples, "Why does your teacher eat with tax collectors and sinners?" He heard this and said, "Those who are well do not need a physician, but the sick do. Go and learn the meaning of the words, 'I desire mercy, not sacrifice.' I did not come to call the righteous but sinners."

St. Bede said of Matthew's conversion,

Our Lord summoned Matthew by speaking to him in words. By an invisible, interior impulse which flooded his mind with the light of grace, the Lord instructed him to walk in his own footsteps. In this way, Matthew came to understand that Christ, who was summoning him away from earthly possessions, had incorruptible treasures of heaven in his gift.[113]

Ah, that we can relate to! We don't have to be wealthy to compare gifts from Christ to "gifts" the world has to offer. Rich or poor, every life offers temptations and idols. Ask yourself, "Where do my earthly possessions fit into the path I'm walking? Am I willing to drop everything, as Matthew did, to follow Jesus? Do I listen every day to the 'invisible, interior impulse' that can flood my mind with the light of grace and beckon me to belief?"

To Ponder or Do

- The Lord called Matthew to mercy and a new life, and "leaving everything behind, [Matthew] got up and followed him" (Luke 5:28). God has called you as well. Consider the ways his call has revealed his mercy in your life. How have you allowed that mercy to overflow to others?

- When scribes and Pharisees asked Jesus' disciples why their leader ate with tax collectors and sinners, Jesus responded that those who are well don't need a physician, but rather, the sick do. He came to call sinners, he told them, not the righteous.

The minute we start thinking that sinners are "others" or that we're hanging out in the righteous zone, we probably need to get to Confession. If you haven't been to Confession in a while, drop by or make an appointment with your priest.

- At his general audience in St. Peter's Square on April 13, 2016, Pope Francis focused on the call of Matthew:

By calling Matthew, Jesus shows sinners that he does not look at their past, at their social condition, at external conventions, but rather opens up a new future for them. I once heard a beautiful saying: "There is no saint without a past and there is no sinner without a future." This is what Jesus does. . . . It is enough to respond to the invitation with a humble and sincere heart. The Church is not a community of perfect ones, but of disciples on a journey, who follow the Lord because they recognize themselves as sinners and in need of his forgiveness. The Christian life is therefore a school of humility that opens us to grace.[114]

The quotation echoes Oscar Wilde, a prodigal son who converted to Catholicism on his deathbed. A character in Wilde's play *A Woman of No Importance* says that the only difference between the saint and the sinner is that every saint has a past, and every sinner has a future.

Jesus opens the possibility of a new future to everyone. Is there someone in your life with "a past"? Do you know someone striving for a new future? Say a prayer for them today.

Pray

Lord Jesus, help me keep my life in perspective. I don't want to own more than I need, and I don't want to overvalue what I have. Please help me strike the right balance. St. Matthew, pray for me. Help me continually reexamine my earthly attachments and learn how to detach from anything that stands between you, Jesus, and me.

September 29

STS. MICHAEL, GABRIEL, AND RAPHAEL, ARCHANGELS (MICHAELMAS)

Connect

Traditionally we think of Michael as protector, Gabriel as messenger, and Raphael as healer. With a trio like this in our corner, we can conquer in battle, listen for God's messages, and accept his healing balm in times of trouble.

Michael is mentioned twice in the Book of Daniel and twice in the Book of Revelation. In Daniel he is described as "the great prince, guardian of your people" (12:1). In Revelation 12:7-9, we see Michael battling against the dragon, expelling him from heaven and throwing him "down to earth" (12:9). His power is immense.

Gabriel also appears in the Book of Daniel (see 8:15-27 and 9:21-27), helping Daniel understand the visions he's been granted. Gabriel delivered all kinds of good news. He told Zechariah that he and his wife, Elizabeth, would have a son, John, who would prepare the people for the Lord (see Luke 1:11-20). Gabriel's most famous announcement was to Mary, in Luke 1:28: "Hail, full of grace, the Lord is with you!" (RSVCE).

Raphael, whose name translates to "God heals," appears in the Book of Tobit. He is the angel who removes the scales from Tobit's eyes, restores his vision, and binds a demon, thus allowing Tobit's son, Tobias, to marry Sarah (see Tobit 3:7-17).

These specific stories of angelic intervention point to God's personal involvement in our lives. He loves us enough to send angels. That's a weighty truth to contemplate.

To Ponder or Do

- In his Morning Meditation on June 9, 2017, Pope Francis gave some "advice for the weekend." He recommended taking fifteen minutes to read the Book of Tobit and search for parallels in our own lives. "Our life," said the Holy Father, "journeys between bad times and times of weakness, but the Lord is always there. . . . Do I know how to discern the Lord's presence, to turn to him in prayer? And then in praise, in the beautiful moments, the praise of joy, to thank him for what has happened?"[115]

- Have you ever felt protection, sensed a "message," or been healed in a way that felt like divine intervention? Though we may not have seen or heard divine messengers, we know that angels are real. Ask St. Raphael to pray today for someone you know who needs or desires healing.

- If you haven't given them much thought, read up on angels. An inspiring piece from The Word Among Us website points out a simple but startling difference between angels and human beings:

What's more, we can do something the angels can't. We can actually receive Jesus as our nourishment. All the qualities of God that the angels share—his wisdom, love, and beauty—are contained in the Eucharist. And that's what we are privileged to take into our very bodies! There is nothing more inspiring than to see that God loves us enough to share his very life with us. The next time you attend Mass, know that you are in the company of angels, and join them in giving him all the praise and worship your heart can muster![116]

Pray

Lord, sometimes you care for me in roundabout, inexplicable, or invisible ways. You protect me, speak to me, and heal me, both directly and through the heavenly beings you created. Help me be aware of the presence of these powerful beings and ask for their intercession every day. Sts. Michael, Gabriel, and Raphael, pray for me!

September 30

ST. JEROME (C. 345–420)

Priest, Doctor of the Church; patron of librarians, translators, students, archivists, Scripture scholars

Born in what is now Croatia, St. Jerome was educated in Rome. He is famous for translating the Bible from Hebrew and Greek into Latin, giving the Church a universal version of Scripture. Known as the Vulgate (*editio vulgata*—basically, the "common version"), Jerome's translation superseded the many Latin versions circulating at the time. His biblical commentaries are still studied today.

Despite his deep faith, his fervor, and his dazzling intellect, Jerome was an abrasive guy. Simply put, he sometimes couldn't keep his mouth shut. In his typical outspoken fashion, he said of his contemporary St. Ambrose, "I withhold judgment of him because he is still alive, fearing either to praise or blame lest, in one event, I should be blamed for adulation, and, in the other, for speaking the truth."[117]

Jerome's bluntness, rudeness, and unfiltered approach to nearly everyone and everything make him one of those saints many of us can relate to as we strive for holiness. Was he imperfect? Definitely. Was he deeply in love with God? Yes.

- If we are "outspoken" in the same way Jerome was, do we tend to elevate this trait and consider it a strength? Or are we able to recognize when our blunt speech is in fact a fault? We don't have to be perfect; we simply have to want the perfection that life with the Lord offers. We are all rough gems, in need of polishing if we are to be gleaming diamonds. What's the rough spot you continually polish?

It is no small gain to know your own ignorance.

—St. Jerome[118]

October

THE ROSARY

It's the month of the Rosary.

You might be saying, "I love the Rosary," or you may be groaning, "I can't get through the Rosary without falling asleep!" Never fear. St. Thérèse of Lisieux, whose feast day is October 1, said,

> [W]hen alone (I am ashamed to admit it) the recitation of the Rosary is more difficult for me than the wearing of an instrument of penance. . . . I force myself in vain to meditate on the mysteries of the rosary; I don't succeed in fixing my mind on them. For a long time I was desolate about this lack of devotion which astonished me, for I love the Blessed Virgin so much that it should be easy for me to recite in her honor prayers which are so pleasing to her. Now I am less desolate; I think that the Queen of heaven, since she is my Mother, must see my good will and she is satisfied with it.[119]

Some saints were devoted to the Rosary, some struggled with it, and some never really talked about it at all. Wherever you are with the Rosary, it's okay. Whether you pray it every

day, tiptoe toward it, and then back away or turn to it in times of trouble, it's all good. The Rosary is not a requirement for heaven, but it can be a great way to talk to Mary and to meditate on the mysteries of the faith.

Pray

Mother Mary, Queen of Heaven, every time I pray this month, please see my goodwill, be satisfied with it, and know that I love you. Please carry my petitions to your son.

"Holy Mary, Mother of God, pray for us sinners, now and at the hour of our death. Amen."

Liturgical Color

Green, for Ordinary Time

A Peek into October's Possibilities

OCTOBER 1
Memorial of St. Thérèse of Lisieux

OCTOBER 2
Memorial of the Guardian Angels

OCTOBER 3
Optional Memorial of St. Theodora Guerin

OCTOBER 4
Memorial of St. Francis of Assisi

OCTOBER 5
Optional Memorial of St. Maria Faustina Kowalska

OCTOBER 7
Memorial of Our Lady of the Rosary

OCTOBER 15
Memorial of St. Teresa of Jesus

OCTOBER 18
Feast of St. Luke the Evangelist

October 1

Religious, Doctor of the Church;
patron of missionaries and florists

This patron saint of missionaries never had the chance to spread the gospel by traveling the world, but her reach is nevertheless without limits. St. Thérèse, also known by her religious name, Thérèse of the Child Jesus and the Holy Face, entered Lisieux's Carmelite convent—where two of her sisters were already nuns—when she was only fifteen. She spent the next nine years there, perfecting her "little way" of holiness before dying of tuberculosis. This little way, accessible to all, involves nothing more than hidden, daily, and humble acts of charity that, carried out to a heroic degree, can lead anyone to perfection.

Thérèse sometimes referred to herself as God's "little flower," a nickname that has contributed to a misinterpretation of her as a woman of mousy mildness. On the contrary, her strength was without question. Not only did she practice her little way with extraordinary heroism, but she also suffered horrifically in the year preceding her death as tuberculosis ate away at her. Her superior forbade pain medication because she felt that Thérèse, as a religious, ought to be able to take the pain.

In the end, however, Thérèse's worst suffering came from a dark night that descended during her last few months. "God allowed my soul to be overrun by an impenetrable darkness," she wrote. "I get tired of the darkness all around me, [and the voice which says] death will make nonsense of your hopes; it will only mean a night darker than ever, the night of mere non-existence."[120]

Thérèse wrote her posthumously published autobiography, *The Story of a Soul*, at the command of her superiors. They unfortunately allowed Thérèse's sister and others to heavily edit the work, to conform more closely to a pious ideal. Nevertheless, they left Thérèse's message intact, and the work went on to reach millions. Now restored to Thérèse's original manuscript, the story continues to inspire and encourage today.

In many ways, Thérèse can be considered a heavenly companion for those who feel lost, abandoned, in despair, or in spiritual darkness. For all of us, her little way of offering every act to God, no matter how small, is equal parts doable and daunting.

- Before she died, Thérèse promised to send showers of roses to those who sought her intercession. When my husband was on his journey to the Catholic Church, my spiritual director and I prayed to St. Thérèse. Imagine my surprise when my husband and I moved into a new house and discovered a rosebush in the backyard, a bush my husband almost cut down but didn't, "for some strange reason," he said. Tom came into the Church the next year. Have you ever asked St. Thérèse for a sign of roses?

This daring ambition of aspiring to great sanctity has never left me. I don't rely on my own merits, because I haven't any; I put all my confidence in him who is virtue, who is holiness itself.

—St. Thérèse of Lisieux[121]

October 2

THE GUARDIAN ANGELS

Celebrate your guardian angel today!
As Pope Francis said,

Our angel is not only with us; he also sees God the Father. He is in relationship with Him. He is the daily bridge, from the moment we arise to the moment we go to bed. He accompanies us and is a link between us and God the Father. The angel is the daily gateway to transcendence, to the encounter with the Father: that is, the angel helps me to go forward because he looks upon the Father, and he knows the way. Let us not forget these companions along the journey.[122]

Prayers to our guardian angel aren't just for kids. Talk to your angel today and every day, using one of these traditional prayers:

Angel of God, my guardian dear,
to whom God's love commits me here,
ever this day be at my side,
to light and guard, to rule and guide. Amen.

O my good Angel,
whom God, by his divine mercy,
has appointed to be my guardian,
enlighten and protect me,
direct and govern me this day. Amen.

If you find it impossible to pray, hide behind your good Angel and charge him to pray in your stead.

—St. John Vianney[123]

October 3

ST. THÉODORE GUÉRIN
(1798–1856)

Religious, founder of the Sisters of Providence of Saint Mary-of-the-Woods; patron of Lafayette Diocese in Indiana

Anne-Thérèse, born in Etables, France, had a happy family life during her early years. But when she was fifteen, thieves murdered her father, a sailor, as he made his way home on furlough. Anne-Thérèse took care of her mother, who sank into depression, and her younger sister, putting on hold her desire to enter the convent. Her mother eventually allowed her to follow her vocation. When she was twenty-five, Ann-Thérèse joined the Sisters of Providence, taking the name Theodore.

After seventeen years as a sister and teacher, Sr. Théodore was asked by her superior to lead a group of sisters to America to teach and care for the poor and sick. Sr. Théodore's spirited, attractive personality shines out even today from her animated journal entries and the thousands of letters she wrote over the years. Her fellow religious failed to appreciate her style, however, replying to her letter detailing the ocean voyage to America: "We have read your little account of the voyage with interest but to be frank, . . . we would have preferred it if you had written in a style less romantic and more pious."[124]

In Indiana, Guérin and the other sisters battled not only poverty but also cruelty from anti-Catholic settlers, who may have set the fire that burned down the sisters' barns. A corrupt and impossible bishop competed with Guérin for control of the Sisters of Providence of Saint Mary-of-the-Woods. She remained patient and steadfast, even when, on one occasion, he locked her up while he went off to enjoy a meal. Mother Guérin persevered, Rome replaced the bishop, and her order grew and blossomed as the sisters established schools, orphanages, and even pharmacies.

- Mother Guérin had to endure many trials, but her trust in God's providence never wavered. Have you ever had to blindly trust that God was still steering the boat when you were traveling in stormy waters? Does that level of trust come easily to you?

At each step we can admire the grandeur, the power, the goodness of God.

—St. Mother Théodore Guérin[125]

Pilgrimage Alert

Saint Mary-of-the-Woods, in western Indiana, is the home of the Sisters of Providence. Find out more about visiting the Shrine of Saint Mother Théodore Guérin at spsmw.org.

October 4

ST. FRANCIS OF ASSISI
(C. 1182–1226)

Religious, founder of the Franciscan order; patron of animals, ecology, and merchants; and copatron, with St. Catherine of Siena, of Italy

Francis, beloved for his complete abandonment to God, once said, "I do not want to hear any mention of the rule of St. Augustine, of St. Bernard, or of St. Benedict. The Lord has told me that he wanted to make a new fool of me."[126]

Pope Francis took his name from this great saint of Assisi, who was devoted to poverty and to people. As G. K. Chesterton said, "He was a lover of God and he was really and truly a lover of men; possibly a much rarer mystical vocation."[127] St. Francis was also the inspiration for Pope Francis' encyclical letters *Laudato Si* [On Care for Our Common Home] and *Fratelli Tutti* [On Fraternity and Social Friendship].

Born into a wealthy merchant family, Francis was a good businessman as well as a leader of the partying young men of the town. "A cautious businessman," said an early biographer, "but a very showy spender."[128] He went to war, presumably looking for adventure, but was taken prisoner for a year. After his release, he was sick for another year, and he soon found himself disillusioned, no longer content with the things of the world.

Francis had a dream in which Christ called him to "follow the master rather than the man."[129] He began to devote himself to prayer and, overcoming his revulsion, visited leper houses. He rejected material goods and his role in the family business, stripping off his clothes, in a famous incident, to return them to his mortified father.

While in the Church of San Damiano in 1206, Francis heard Jesus speak to him from the crucifix: "Francis, go repair my church, which as you can see is in ruin."[130] Francis took the message literally, and he went to work repairing three nearby run-down churches. But God had bigger plans, and ultimately Francis set a new religious order in motion, dedicated to poverty and preaching the gospel.

Devoted to Christ in the Eucharist, Francis modeled and encouraged a warm and personal spirituality that breathed new life into religious practice. He received the stigmata, the five wounds of Christ, but humble as always, he tried to hide this divine gift even as he endured the pain that accompanied it.

Francis suffered from numerous illnesses in his final two years. He died in 1226, at the age of forty-five, surrounded by his brothers. "I have done my part," he told them. "May Christ teach you to do yours."[131] When Pope Gregory IX canonized Francis two years later, the pope was moved to tears speaking about the beloved fool for Christ.

- Francis had known wealth and rejected it, leading many to consider him a fool. In what ways do you think of yourself as a "fool for Christ"?

Pray

A Prayer to the Creator

Lord, Father of our human family,
you created all human beings equal in dignity:
pour forth into our hearts a fraternal spirit
and inspire in us a dream of renewed encounter,
dialogue, justice and peace.
Move us to create healthier societies
and a more dignified world,
a world without hunger, poverty, violence and war.

May our hearts be open
to all the peoples and nations of the earth.
May we recognize the goodness and beauty
that you have sown in each of us,
and thus forge bonds of unity, common projects,
and shared dreams. Amen.

—Pope Francis, *Fratelli Tutti*[132]

October 5

ST. MARIA FAUSTINA KOWALSKA
(1905–1938)

Religious, mystic

It's a story that seems common among women saints: young Faustina wanted to become a nun, but her parents initially forbade it. Discouraged, Faustina went to work as a maid to help support her family. But something happened that demonstrated how mistaken her parents had been.

In 1924 Faustina experienced her first vision of Jesus while she was at a dance with her sister. The suffering Lord appeared and called to her, bidding her to go to Warsaw. She obeyed, and there, after being turned away from several orders, she joined the Sisters of Our Lady of Mercy.

Faustina's visions of heaven, hell, and the merciful Christ became frequent and vivid. After extensive psychological testing, her spiritual directors believed her and encouraged her to record the messages she received from Jesus. These can be succinctly summarized: God's mercy is here for all. Sr. Faustina promoted devotion to Divine Mercy through both its feast day and the Novena to Divine Mercy, which is meant to precede the feast.

Fr. Michael Sopoćko, Faustina's confessor, introduced her to Eugeniusz Marcin Kazimirowski, the Polish artist who would paint Faustina's vision of the Divine Mercy of Jesus in 1934. It is the well-known image we still see today.

At her canonization Mass on April 30, 2000, Pope John Paul II said,

> Today my joy is truly great in presenting the life and witness of *Sr. Faustina Kowalska* to the whole Church as a gift from God for our time.. By divine Providence, the life of this humble daughter of Poland was completely linked with the history of the 20th century, the century we have just left behind. In fact, it was between the First and Second World Wars that Christ entrusted his message of mercy to her. Those who remember, who were witnesses and participants in the events of those years and the horrible sufferings they caused for millions of people, know well how necessary was the message of mercy.[133]

- I have been personally touched by the Divine Mercy devotion, ever since a friend suggested the chaplet to me during a difficult time in my life. After praying it for a month, a seemingly impossible situation turned around. If you have ever prayed the chaplet, you've felt its power. If you haven't, do yourself a favor, and give this devotion a try. God's mercy is overflowing.

Humanity will not find peace until it turns trustfully to divine mercy.

—Jesus to Sister Faustina, as recorded in her diary [134]

PILGRIMAGE ALERT

Visit the National Shrine of the Divine Mercy in Stockbridge, Massachusetts. Find out more about it at shrineofdivinemercy.org.

October 7

OUR LADY OF THE ROSARY

Connect

When I first became a Catholic, the Rosary was foreign to me. I wasn't used to praying to Mary, I wondered about the repetitive nature and efficacy of this prayer, and I worried about doing it wrong. It took time to ease into it.

What made my relationship with the Rosary grow? My relationship with *Mary* grew. It happened in stages, over months and years. But one day, I realized that in praying the Rosary, I was simply asking my mother to pray for me. Even when I threw out a lone desperate Hail Mary, I was asking her to be in my corner.

In contemplating the mysteries of the Rosary, we are meditating on the saving beauty of Christ's life. Blessed Bartolo Longo, known as the "Apostle of the Rosary," was a former satanist who converted and was ordained a Catholic priest. He said,

The Rosary is a teacher of life, a teacher full of gentleness and love, where people beneath the gaze of Mary, almost without noticing, discover they are being slowly educated in preparation for the second life, that which is authentic life, for it is not destined to end in a very few years, but to go on unto eternity.[135]

And as Pope John Paul II wrote, "To recite the Rosary is nothing other than to *contemplate with Mary the face of Christ*."[136]

To Ponder or Do

- Do you pray the Rosary regularly, sometimes, occasionally, or never? Praying the Rosary is not an article of faith, and it's not required for your salvation. If you love the Rosary, take a moment to thank God for the gift of sinking deeply into this ancient form of prayer. If you aren't sure how you feel about the Rosary, take comfort in the knowledge that Mary sees your goodwill for what it is. Just talk to her, and let her know what you think and how you feel.

- If you pray the Rosary regularly but find yourself meditating on the same mysteries each time, try spending time with another set. The mysteries are based in Scripture, and contemplation of them brings us closer to Christ. Whether you pray the Joyful, Luminous, Sorrowful, or Glorious Mysteries, you are contemplating with Mary the face of Christ.

- Just getting started? Pray a decade of the Rosary in the car, on your way to Mass, alone or with your spouse or family.

- Roses! Buy some roses to grace the kitchen table or the living room today. Say a Hail Mary whenever you pass them, and offer your prayers for someone who is struggling with faith.

Pray

Hail, his palace.
Hail, his tabernacle.
Hail, his robe.
Hail, his handmaid.
Hail, his mother.
And hail, all holy virtues,
Who, by the grace and inspiration of the Holy Spirit,
Are poured into the hearts of the faithful
So that, faithless no longer,
They may be made faithful servants of God
Through you. Amen.

—A prayer of St. Francis of Assisi

October 15

ST. TERESA OF ÁVILA (1515–1582)

*Religious, mystic, Doctor of the Church; patron of headache
sufferers, the sick, Spanish Catholic writers*

What an amazing woman! St. Teresa of Ávila, also known as St. Teresa of Jesus, is one of four women to be named Doctors of the Church. She is in the company of St. Thérèse of Lisieux, St. Catherine of Siena, and St. Hildegard of Bingen. If you don't know this powerhouse, befriend her immediately.

At the age of seven, Teresa ran away from home, intent on becoming a martyr to "see God," as she told her parents. A few years later, however, as the pleasures of the world crowded in, this charming, intelligent young woman with a magnetic personality found herself attracted to society, parties, and the flattery that her winning ways invited.

Teresa pursued the religious life, even though she had no strong inclination toward it. In 1536 she entered a Carmelite convent where the environment was relaxed: she had her own suite of rooms and lived in comfort, though the nuns did follow basic patterns of religious life. A severe health crisis brought this low-key lifestyle to an end, and Teresa returned home. After three years of illness, she returned to the convent.

Over the next fifteen years, she took a slow journey into a deep, mystical, and genuine faith.

As Teresa began to live the Carmelite life rigorously, a few other sisters joined her. In 1562 Teresa founded the Convent of St. Joseph at Ávila, there to pursue a more perfect observance of the rule. Eventually this led to the founding of her shoe-shunning order, dubbed the Discalced (barefoot) Carmelites.

The order grew as Teresa traveled around Spain, in appalling conditions, pushing much-needed reform among the Carmelites. She recruited St. John of the Cross to help her. They became allies in the difficult and much-resisted reform of the order.

Like St. Philip Neri, another charming saint blessed with many gifts, Teresa seemed to have it all: holiness, humor—"God, deliver me from sullen saints,"[137] she famously said—and the talents necessary for active ministry, as well as a mystical, contemplative prayer life that kept her close to the Lord. Despite health struggles, she forged on.

Teresa's beautiful and accessible spiritual classics—*The Way of Perfection, The Interior Castle,* and her autobiography— continue to be read by millions. Pope Paul VI declared her a Doctor of the Church in 1970.

- No matter what your tendency—active, contemplative, or somewhere in between—St. Teresa is your go-to. Ask her to pray for you and for the development of your many gifts. Laugh with her today about the challenge of dealing with "sullen saints," and thank God for the gift of laughter.

Let nothing disturb you,
Let nothing frighten you,
All things are passing away:
God never changes.
Patience obtains all things.
Whoever has God lacks nothing;
God alone suffices.

—St. Teresa of Ávila[138]

October 18

ST. LUKE THE EVANGELIST

Connect

Tradition tells us that Luke was probably a physician, possibly an artist, and the author of one of the three synoptic ("through the same eye") Gospels, as well as of the Acts of the Apostles. He was a companion to Paul in his missionary work and the only Gentile among the Gospel writers. His Gospel is generally considered to be the "Gospel of Mercy" or the "Gospel of the Poor," as he strove to communicate to other Gentiles who Jesus really is and what he has accomplished: he died and rose for Gentiles as well as for Jews.

Luke's emphasis on conversion and mercy surfaces again and again. Only in the Gospel of Luke do we meet the sinful woman who anointed Jesus' feet (see 7:36-50), read about the woman's lost coin (15:8-10), and encounter the prodigal son (15:11-32) and the good thief (23:39-43). Through Luke's eyes, we repeatedly see the joy of God when even a single sinner repents.

And it's in the Gospel of Luke that we read of the angel Gabriel's appearances to Zechariah, the annunciation to Mary, her Magnificat, and Simeon's canticle ("Now, Lord, you may dismiss your servant") (see Luke 1 and 2).

Scholars have noted the prominent place women hold in Luke's Gospel and his emphasis on the role of the Holy Spirit in both his Gospel and the Acts of the Apostles. Read his treatment of the descent of the Holy Spirit at Pentecost (see Acts 2), and invite the Holy Spirit to enkindle the fire of his love within you and give hope to the Church as the Spirit continues to guide it.

To Ponder or Do

- Read through the Scripture passages mentioned above. What in particular jumps out at you or speaks to you?

- When you read the parable of the prodigal son, with whom do you identify more: the prodigal son or the faithful older brother who never left home? In his book *Jesus of Nazareth*, Pope Benedict XVI wrote of the older brother's point of view:

He sees only injustice. And this betrays the fact that he too had secretly dreamed of a freedom without limits, that his obedience has made him inwardly bitter, and that he has no awareness of the grace of being at home, of the true freedom that he enjoys as a son.[139]

Does this change the way you view the parable?

- Do you ever pray the Liturgy of the Hours (also known as the Divine Office and commonly referred to as the breviary)? Consider checking out the various ways you can access and pray the prayers that religious and many laity the world over pray daily as a way to mark and sanctify each portion of the day. There are apps, such as iBreviary, that make it easy to dive in.

Pray

Lord, my soul magnifies you, and my spirit rejoices in you. You who are mighty have done great things for me. Holy is your name.

Thank you for treasuring me, Father. I can't fully fathom your love, but I am grateful that you love me: a sinful woman, a lost coin, a prodigal child, a repentant thief. Thank you, my God and my Savior!

November

THE HOLY SOULS
IN PURGATORY

It's the month of saints, all souls, and prayers for the holy souls in purgatory.

It's fitting that in the final leg of the liturgical year, we focus on the "last things." We take time to rejoice in and with our heavenly role models on November 1, the Solemnity of All Saints. On November 2, All Souls Day, we honor all the dead, and throughout the month, we pray for souls in purgatory.

In his Angelus address of November 1, 2020, Pope Francis said,

> The Saints and the Blesseds are the most authoritative witnesses of Christian hope, because they lived it fully in their existence, amidst joys and sufferings, carrying out *the Beatitudes* that Jesus preached and that today resound in the Liturgy (cf. Mt 5:1-12a). The evangelical Beatitudes, in fact, are the way to holiness.[140]

Let's continue on that way together, as we honor, emulate, and pray for those who came before us.

Pray

Eternal Father, I offer you the most Precious Blood of your divine Son, Jesus, in union with the Masses said throughout the world today, for all the holy souls in purgatory, for sinners everywhere, for sinners in the universal Church, those in my own home and within my family. Amen.

 —Prayer of St. Gertrude: Releasing Souls from Purgatory[141]

Liturgical Color

Green for Ordinary Time
Purple on the First Sunday in Advent

A Peek into November's Possibilities

NOVEMBER 1
Solemnity of All Saints

NOVEMBER 2
Commemoration of the Faithful Departed (All Souls' Day)

NOVEMBER 8
Optional Memorial of St. Elizabeth of the Trinity

NOVEMBER 13
Memorial of St. Frances Xavier Cabrini

NOVEMBER 16
Optional Memorial of St. Gertrude the Great

NOVEMBER 21
Memorial of the Presentation of the Blessed Virgin Mary

November 1

Connect

Today we celebrate all the saints in heaven: those the Church has formally recognized and named through canonization or beatification, and the many other souls—nameless, unknown, ordinary people like us—who are in the presence of God. It's a day of hope in Christ and hope in the resurrection. And as Pope Francis said, the Beatitudes are the "path to holiness," so today is a beautiful day to spend some time with them:

> Blessed are the poor in spirit,
>   for theirs is the kingdom of heaven.
> Blessed are they who mourn,
>   for they will be comforted.
> Blessed are the meek,
>   for they will inherit the land.

Blessed are they who hunger and thirst for righteousness,
  for they will be satisfied.
Blessed are the merciful,
  for they will be shown mercy.
Blessed are the clean of heart,
  for they will see God.
Blessed are the peacemakers,
  for they will be called children of God.
Blessed are they who are persecuted for the sake of righteousness,
  for theirs is the kingdom of heaven. (Matthew 5:3-10)

To Ponder or Do

- Consider these words from Pope Francis' Angelus address on this feast day in 2020, and remember that you are walking toward heaven in your own "unique way, an unrepeatable way," and that you have your own "variety of gifts and real life stories."

Today's solemnity that honors All Saints reminds us of the personal and universal vocation to holiness, and proposes sure models for this journey that each person walks in a unique way, an unrepeatable way. It is enough to think of the inexhaustible variety of gifts and real life stories there are among the saints: they are not all the same, each one has their own personality, and developed their own life of holiness according to their own personality. Each one of us can do it, take this path: meekness, meekness, please, and we will head toward holiness.[142]

- Do you enjoy crafts with kids? There are a million ideas waiting for you online, such as Alice Gunther's "spoon saints." Give the kids some wooden ice cream spoons, yarn, fabric, markers, and glue, and let them create the cutest cloud of witnesses you'll see this side of heaven.

- Have a special meal tonight, and define it in your own "unique way, an unrepeatable way." Maybe for you, "special" means pizza delivery, a gluten-free feast, a bowl of cereal for the sheer ease, or picking up every family member's favorite takeout from different restaurants. Be a unique saint tonight.

- If you had to name the saint you most identify with, who would it be? If you had to choose just one saint to emulate for the rest of your life, who would that be? Are they the same saint?

Pray

Lord, I don't usually feel like a saint. Remind me that those we venerate today usually didn't "feel it" either. Help me face each and every day's challenges as the saints did: by putting all my trust and hope in you and moving forward one step at a time.

For I know the plans I have for you, says the LORD, plans for welfare and not for evil, to give you a future and a hope. (Jeremiah 29:11, RSVCE)

November 2

COMMEMORATION OF ALL THE FAITHFUL DEPARTED (ALL SOULS' DAY)

Connect

The act of praying for the dead can seem strange, but it makes wonderful logical sense. As the *Catechism of the Catholic Church* says:

> All who die in God's grace and friendship, but still imperfectly purified, are indeed assured of their eternal salvation; but after death they undergo purification, so as to achieve the holiness necessary to enter the joy of heaven. (1030)

Most of us will be in need of that cleansing bath before we enter into the presence of God and the intensity of his light. The Church teaches that we help each other in this regard, praying for one another, through our bond in the communion of saints:

> [A] perennial link of charity exists between the faithful who have already reached their heavenly home, those who are expiating their sins in purgatory and those who are still pilgrims on earth. Between them there is, too, an abundant exchange

of all good things. (*Catechism* 1475, quoting Pope Paul VI, *Indulgentiarum Doctrina*, 5)

 In other words, we're here for each other, whether we're on earth, in purgatory, or in heaven. We are eternally connected. Praying for the departed is a privilege. We can hope that others will pray for us when we depart this earth as well.

To Ponder or Do

- Add this short prayer after every meal blessing:

Eternal rest grant unto them, O Lord.
And let the perpetual light shine upon them.
And may the souls of all the faithful departed, through the mercy of God, rest in peace. Amen.

- Visit the cemetery. Record in a journal or post prominently somewhere in your home the names of the departed for whom you want to pray this month.

- Pray the Litany for the Holy Souls in Purgatory, which begins with these words:

O Jesus, you suffered and died that all mankind might be saved and brought to eternal happiness. Hear our pleas for further mercy on the souls of:

My dear parents and grandparents, my Jesus, mercy!
My brothers and sisters and other near relatives, my Jesus, mercy!
My godparents and sponsors of confirmation, my Jesus, mercy!
My spiritual and temporal benefactors, my Jesus, mercy!
My friends and neighbors, my Jesus, mercy!
All for whom love or duty bids me pray, my Jesus, mercy!
Those who have offended me, my Jesus, mercy!
Those who have suffered disadvantage or harm through me,
my Jesus, mercy!
(The full litany can be found online.)

- C. S. Lewis's explanation of purgatory, in his *Letters to Malcolm*, offers insight into why purgatory makes a great deal of sense:

Our souls demand Purgatory, don't they? Would it not break the heart if God said to us, "It is true, my son, that your breath smells and your rags drip with mud and slime, but we are charitable here and no one will upbraid you with these things, nor draw away from you. Enter into the joy"? Should we not reply, "With submission, sir, and if there is no objection, I'd *rather* be cleaned first." "It may hurt, you know"—"Even so, sir."[143]

Pray

Thank you, Lord, for the communion of saints. The connections among the pilgrim Church on earth, the penitent Church in purgatory, and the triumphant Church in heaven are beyond my comprehension but not beyond my grasp. Remind me today that I'm part of this extraordinary communion of saints. "My Jesus, mercy!"

November 8

ST. ELIZABETH OF THE TRINITY
(1880–1906)

*Religious, mystic, writer; patron of the sick,
loss of parents, against illness*

Another Carmelite to admire and celebrate this month! Elizabeth of the Trinity was a devotee of St. Thérèse of Lisieux. Like Thérèse, Elizabeth had a lively and fiery temper when she was young, but she channeled her passionate energy into her love for the Lord. Also like Thérèse, she yearned to enter a Carmelite convent in her early teens, but Elizabeth's mother persuaded her to wait until she was twenty-one. A talented pianist and singer, Elizabeth was a catch, but despite the constant pressure to marry, she was laser focused on religious life.

In 1901 Elizabeth entered the Carmelite convent in Dijon, France. Devoted to the Blessed Trinity, she united herself to the suffering Christ, developed a mystical prayer life, and in obedience to her superior, collected and transcribed her notes on the spiritual life. When she was twenty-three, she was diagnosed with an autoimmune disorder, Addison's Disease, and she died three years later. Her last words were "I am going to Light, to Love, to Life!"[144]

Pope Francis canonized Elizabeth in 2016 after a woman who had sought her intercession was miraculously healed from Sjogren's Syndrome, another autoimmune disease. Like St. Thérèse, St. Elizabeth wanted to spend her heaven doing good on earth. She said,

> I think that in Heaven my mission will be to draw souls by helping them go out of themselves to cling to God by a wholly simple and loving movement, and to keep them in this great silence within that will allow God to communicate Himself to them and transform them into Himself.[145]

- Have you ever had to cling to God with a "wholly simple and loving movement"? Were you able to maintain interior silence during that time? Did you feel that God communicated with you, or did you feel that you had to go forward by blind faith?

O my God, Trinity whom I adore, let me entirely forget myself that I may abide in you, still and peaceful as if my soul were already in eternity; let nothing disturb my peace nor separate me from you, O my unchanging God.

—From St. Elizabeth's Prayer to the Trinity[146]

November 13

ST. FRANCES XAVIER CABRINI
(1850–1917)

Religious, founder;
patron of immigrants and hospital administrators

Relentless. That's what St. Frances Xavier Cabrini was when it came to helping others and saving souls. She was born in Italy, entered religious life there, became a U.S. citizen in 1909, and was the first American citizen to be canonized.

Though Frances was denied entry into the Daughters of the Sacred Heart because of her health, she began teaching and working at an orphanage in Italy. She proved herself more than capable when she took over the management of the orphanage, which had been horribly run. She longed to be a missionary—her goal was to serve in China—and in 1880 she founded the Missionary Sisters of the Sacred Heart.

Sr. Frances' bishop encouraged her, and Pope Leo XIII approved the order, telling Frances that her mission would be "not to the East, but to the West."[147] America would be her China. This approval marked Frances as a trailblazer. Up until that time, the Church regarded missionary work as suitable for men but not women.

Though Frances was initially disappointed when she was sent to America instead of China, she was tireless in her missionary work. "Unstoppable" might be another apt description of this woman who—in spite of lifelong poor health and the anti-Catholic, anti-immigrant prejudice she encountered—traveled to the U.S., Central and South America, England, France, and Italy, leaving hospitals, schools, and convents in her trail. Though at times she erred on the side of rigidity, such as denying admission to her school of children born outside of marriage, Frances overcame the constant obstacles that blocked her way and her work.

Frances died of malaria at the age of sixty-seven, after founding sixty-seven institutions and giving education, health care, material means, and a voice to numerous underserved populations, especially Italian immigrants. In her determination and in the people she served, she brings to mind a line from the musical *Hamilton*: "Immigrants: we get the job done!"

- Mother Frances Cabrini's dogged determination shines forth. When you consider obstacles you've had to overcome, what or who comes to mind? Most of us can't point to a bishop or pope as our personal encourager, but we all have someone who cheers us on against seemingly impossible odds. Who's your number-one encourager?

My Jesus, I have not always recognized your loving plans for me. Every day, with the help of your light, I learn more of your loving care. Continue to increase my awareness of the gentleness of your loving plans. I want to follow the purpose for which I was created. See, I am in your hands. I need you to help me choose the best way to serve you. Walk with me, Jesus. Stay by my side and guide me!

—A Discernment Prayer by Mother Cabrini[148]

PILGRIMAGE ALERT

Are you in Colorado? The beautiful Mother Cabrini Shrine in Golden awaits you. Find out more at mothercabrinishrine. org. If you're near Chicago, plan to spend some time at The National Shrine of St. Frances Xavier Cabrini. Visit their website at cabrininationalshrine.org.

November 16

ST. GERTRUDE THE GREAT
(C. 1256–1302)

Religious, mystic, theologian; patron of the West Indies

A Benedictine nun and a woman of vast intellect, Gertrude the Great is one of the great mystics of the Middle Ages. We know very little about her family and childhood, although it seems that she grew up in a monastery in Germany headed by Abbess Gertrude of Hackerborn. The younger sister of the abbess, St. Mechtilde, cared for the child Gertrude and became a strong influence on her spirituality.

Highly educated, Gertrude enjoyed pursuing knowledge for its own sake but later considered her thirst for academics to be empty and vain. What an interesting contrast to Edith

Stein, who grew to see her academic pursuits as a way to serve God! Another marvelous example of the diversity of the saints.

Gertrude experienced her first visions of the Lord when she was twenty-five. In one of them, she saw him as a young man with wounds on his hands, taking her hand and leading her from the trappings of her earthly attachments. Such profound, intimate encounters were formative, and they continued until her death at forty-five. They led her to adopt a new mission: to transform what she learned and experienced of the Lord in her visions into a common language she could share with others.

As Pope Benedict XVI said, "[S]he devoted herself to writing and popularizing the truth of faith with clarity and simplicity, with grace and persuasion, serving the Church faithfully and lovingly so as to be helpful to and appreciated by theologians and devout people."[149]

Most of St. Gertrude's works are lost to us, but we still have *The Herald of Divine Love*, *The Revelations,* and *Spiritual Exercises*. She is the only female saint to be dubbed "the Great."

St. Gertrude felt a kinship with the holy souls in purgatory and gave us the prayer, found at the beginning of this month, that we still pray for them today.

- Gertrude felt both unworthy of and grateful for the many gifts the Lord bestowed on her. Do you ever struggle to acknowledge and affirm your gifts? None of us, as Gertrude realized, are worthy, but we are all called. Feel comforted, enlightened, and grateful, as Gertrude did.

You flooded me with your gifts, of such beatitude that even were I to live for 1,000 years with no consolation neither interior nor exterior, the memory of them would suffice to comfort me, to enlighten me, to fill me with gratitude.

—St. Gertrude[150]

November 21

FEAST OF THE PRESENTATION OF THE BLESSED VIRGIN MARY IN THE TEMPLE

Connect

This feast originated as early as the sixth century, and Pope Sixtus added it to the universal Church calendar in the fifteenth century. Although there is no scriptural basis for the story, tradition tells us that Mary was consecrated to the Lord when she was a baby and was raised for a time in the Temple. This history of Mary contributes to the portrait of her as a contemplative young woman who was theologically grounded as well as an active believer who lived the day-in, day-out existence of motherhood and family life.

To Ponder or Do

- Pause for a few minutes today to meditate on the meaning of Mary's life as reflected in her presentation. Consider Archbishop William E. Lori's insights from a homily on this feast day:

[A]s we seek to evangelize more vigorously . . . and seek in God's grace to create missionary disciples capable of encountering others and walking with them, leading them to Christ and to the Church, . . . let us hasten in prayer to Mary. . . .

For Mary always leads us to Jesus. It was to this mission that her life was dedicated as she was presented in the Temple. From her parents, Mary learned to trust in God's promise of salvation and to live in faithful expectation that those promises would be fulfilled.[151]

- "Mary Gardens" are an ancient way of honoring the Blessed Mother. It's probably not the time of year for gardening, unless you live in a warm climate. But in the spirit of a Mary Garden, pick up a small bouquet at the store. Enjoy its fragrance and beauty every time you pass it, and thank Mary for saying yes to God's invitation and promise.

- Mary is known by numerous titles: Mother of, Daughter, Lady, Queen, Glory of, Advocate, Comfort of, Vessel, Tabernacle, Seat of . . . the list goes on. Look up "titles of Mary" in the *Catechism of the Catholic*

Church, or just spend a little time searching online. Do you have a favorite "nickname" for the Mystical Rose?

Pray

The *Salve Regina*, "Hail, Holy Queen"

Hail, holy Queen, Mother of mercy, our life, our sweetness and our hope. To thee do we cry, poor banished children of Eve. To thee do we send up our sighs, mourning and weeping in this valley of tears. Turn, then, most gracious advocate, thine eyes of mercy toward us, and after this, our exile, show unto us the blessed fruit of thy womb, Jesus. O clement, O loving, O sweet Virgin Mary.

December

ADVENT AND THE
COMING OF CHRIST

O come, Emmanuel!

Advent heralds the beginning of the new liturgical calendar. It opens with the fourth Sunday before Christmas. The word *advent* derives from the Latin *ad* [to] and *venire* [come], meaning, in terms of the liturgical calendar, a season of quiet, watchful, and hopeful waiting.

Each Advent we're given the chance to contemplate the full mystery of Christ's coming to us: both the first coming of Jesus Christ with a human nature and the second coming of Christ the Messiah at the end of time. These are beautiful and enormous questions to contemplate in these days:

What does it mean that Christ came to us incarnate?

Why as a helpless child?

What does it mean that time will one day end, that Christ will come to us again?

What effects do these extraordinary events of the past and future have on my life, and what does this time of waiting look like for me personally?

Although the world around us launched a Christmas party on Thanksgiving, the Church has other plans. She asks us to slow down and spend the weeks before Christmas mulling and preparing. Historically, Advent was a time of penitential preparation. Although the Church no longer prescribes or requires fasting during this season, we are encouraged to turn inward and cultivate quiet time.

If you have young children, Advent lends itself to activities and saints celebrations that can help them see this as a special time of year—a time set apart to prepare not just for seasonal gift giving but for the greatest gift of all: Jesus. These activities can create a lasting impression, as they help little ones step outside themselves during the countdown to Christmas. Advent wreaths, stories of St. Nicholas as the kids set out shoes on St. Nicholas Eve or of St. Lucy as you celebrate her feast day with St. Lucy's bread—these can shift the focus for children, drawing them into a more faith-filled approach to the big day.

With older and even adult children, the season only grows deeper. We can still light the Advent wreath, but we can also talk about Advent reflections, resolutions, readings, and the great blessing of going to Confession before Christmas. No matter how we observe Advent, let's build on a foundation of immersion in the season. It is the season of watching, waiting, hoping, and also pondering what Mary felt as she anticipated the birth of her child.

Advent is about who Jesus Christ is and why he came to us. Keep your heart set on that truth, and you will be able to put aside stress—or at least manage it—and enjoy calm in this season of hope.

Wherever you are on the path with Christ, be grateful for *this* Advent. Are you single? Newly married? A new mom? Are you crafting an Advent with young children, teens, or grown kids? Are you a widow or an empty nester? Wherever you are, rejoice in this moment. Find time to watch, wait, ponder, plan, and hope, as Mary did. This Advent, let Christ make you new.

Pray

Lord, the beauty of Advent can get lost in the frantically busy days leading up to Christmas. This year help me slow down, savor meaningful moments, and redirect my focus—as many times as I need to—to you. Help me watch and wait and let go of bloated to-do lists and insignificant urgencies. Help me quiet myself as I wait for you to come to me. Lord, help me have hope in you.

Liturgical Color

Purple for the season of Advent
Pink for Gaudete Sunday (the third Sunday of Advent)
White for Christmas

A Peek into December's Possibilities

IDEAS FOR A HOPEFUL ADVENT

DECEMBER 6
Optional Memorial of St. Nicholas

DECEMBER 8
Solemnity of the Immaculate Conception of the Blessed Virgin Mary

DECEMBER 9
Optional Memorial of St. Juan Diego Cuauhtlatoatzin

DECEMBER 12
Feast of Our Lady of Guadalupe

DECEMBER 25
Solemnity of the Nativity of the Lord (Christmas)

DECEMBER 26
Feast of St. Stephen, the first martyr

DECEMBER 27
Feast of St. John the apostle and Evangelist

DECEMBER 28
Feast of the Holy Innocents

IDEAS FOR A HOPEFUL ADVENT

Gather Your Reading

Advent is a marvelous time to dive into some spiritual reading. Is there a particular Catholic work you've been wanting to read? Maybe it's something contemporary or perhaps a spiritual classic. It doesn't have to be a formal or traditional Advent study or devotional. Choose what inspires you, and spend a few minutes a day with a reading that makes you think, helps you pray, or offers you new ideas and insights.

Daily Scripture

Your book for Advent might be the Bible. Check the day's Mass readings, or commit to reading the Gospels. Read a little each day, and don't be afraid to underline and mark up your Bible. God wants us to immerse ourselves in his word.

Set Up a Prayer Spot

Perhaps you did this during Lent, and both the spot and the habit stuck. Or maybe someone else has stolen that corner of the couch that you'd claimed. Either way, pick a spot for Advent, park a prayer book, your Bible, or your Advent reading next to it, and call it yours. Then strive to land there every day. But give yourself grace, knowing that life will throw you "curveballs," and even the best-laid prayer plans sometimes go astray.

Get to Mass or Adoration

Everyone wants to get to Mass a little more often and spend more time with Jesus. The season of Advent includes a holy day of obligation (the Solemnity of the Immaculate Conception), but if you'd like to try going even more often, pick a day of the week, and put it in your planner. Or pick out a couple of favorite feasts or memorials, and commit to getting to Mass on those days. Stop in the church whenever you can for some Adoration time.

Bible Studies

What is your parish offering this season? Are you interested in going and perhaps inviting a friend to join you?

Confession

As with everything else, Confession is much more likely to happen when we put it in the planner. Check your parish's regular and additional Confession times, and make a date for this soul-cleansing sacrament.

Advent Journal

The kids get an Advent calendar—probably one with chocolate—so why not find a daily Advent practice that brings you sweet joy too? Take a little time every day to record what's going on this Advent. Do you have thoughts about a Scripture verse from the Mass readings? Maybe you like to write spontaneously about the season, your family, or your plans. Perhaps that spiritual reading you're delving into deserves to be preserved through quotes and favorite passages copied in your journal.

Grab a piece of chocolate every time you journal.

The Advent Wreath

Do you have one? Do you *want* one? Is the one at Mass enough for you?

You get to decide. Advent wreaths are beautiful, but they aren't required. Maybe you'll plop four chunky candles on a plate or light a simple white candle every night when you sit down to dinner, as a reminder that we are in a special season. Do what works for you.

Look at Lent

Anything that offers growth during Lent works for Advent and any other time of year. Consider a morning offering (see "Observing Lent" for the traditional prayer and a shortened form), praying in new locations, a new or renewed devotion, a daily examen, offering up sufferings, and planning some additional charitable giving.

Make and Destroy a To-Do List (or at Least Part of It)

The weeks leading up to Christmas are full of to-do lists. Make your list, including spiritual, secular, and practical goals. Now look it over with a ruthless eye and a red pen. What *has* to stay? What can go? What would be "nice if you get to it" but not essential?

Now rewrite your to-do list, and divide it into sections: "Personal Spiritual Essentials," "Family/Friend Essentials," "Practical Essentials," and "Nice but Not Necessary Stuff." How much did your list change? Which things on your list can be moved to the *real* Christmas season—between Christmas Day and Epiphany or the Baptism of the Lord—and out of Advent?

Consider the Word "Hope"

What are your hopes for this Advent? Do they involve slowing down or adding new spiritual practices that will draw you closer to God?

Maybe when you think of hope, you simply yearn to feel more optimistic, positive, and loving in the midst of our unsettled world. Write down the word "hope," and post it where you'll see it every day. Every time you notice it, pray, "Jesus, I trust in you."

December 6

ST. NICHOLAS (C. 270-343)

Priest, bishop; patron of children, sailors and travelers, brewers, prisoners and those falsely accused, prostitutes

Though he's a well-loved saint, we actually know very little about Nicholas, bishop of Myra, other than the fact that he was indeed a bishop. Legends have grown up around him, some with elements of the miraculous, such as his raising from the dead three young boys who had been murdered.

Perhaps the best-known story is that of a father who couldn't provide for his three daughters. To save them from forced prostitution, Nicholas anonymously delivered three bags of gold to the family, thus providing a dowry for each of the girls. Some versions of the story have him tossing the bags through the window of the man's house, and others say that he left treasure in the girls' shoes, which were drying outside their home.

This story, tidied up for children's ears, is the basis of traditions of leaving gold coins in children's shoes and other gift giving on this feast day. Behind all the stories about Nicholas is the fact that he loved God wholeheartedly and generously shared everything he had with others.

- This simple but beloved feast day became a firm tradition at our house. Every December 6, my daughters woke up to shoes filled with chocolate coins and other candy, a cute pair of socks, and a shiny new Christmas ornament. It was a small celebration that gave us all huge joy. The generosity of St. Nicholas lives on. How do you observe his day?

[M]aterial generosity—thinking about the poor: "I can give this so that they can eat or have clothes"—has an ulterior result: it enlarges the heart and helps us be magnanimous.
—Pope Francis[152]

December 8

SOLEMNITY OF THE IMMACULATE CONCEPTION OF THE BLESSED VIRGIN MARY

Connect

This feast day refers to Mary herself: *she* was conceived without sin. It does not refer to her conception of Jesus, as many people think.

In 1854, in his papal bull *Ineffabilis Deus,* Pope Pius IX formally defined and declared this doctrine, a long-held belief of the Church:

> Concerning the most Blessed Virgin Mary, Mother of God, ancient indeed is that devotion of the faithful based on the belief that her soul, in the first instant of its creation and in the first instant of the soul's infusion into the body, was, by a special grace and privilege of God, in view of the merits of Jesus Christ, her Son and the Redeemer of the human race, preserved free from all stain of original sin. And in this sense have the faithful ever solemnized and celebrated the Feast of the Conception.[153]

This doctrine is utterly logical and sensible. As Catholic writer Frank Sheed said, "Because He was God, He could give His mother gifts not only before He was born of her, but before she was born herself! This is the meaning of the doctrine of the Immaculate Conception."[154]

God is capable of anything, and why *wouldn't* he want to save his mother from the debilitating effects of original sin? Mary, a human being, needed a savior just as much as we do. In her case, God chose to accomplish his work at her conception. Simple, logical, and beautiful.

To Ponder or Do

- When you go to Mass, thank God for the gift of Mary's immaculate conception, which is a reminder that we are saved not for what we do but by the grace and action of God.

O Mary! From the very first moment of life you were preserved from original sin through the merits of Jesus, whose Mother you were to become. Sin and death have no power over you. From the moment you were conceived, you have enjoyed the unique privilege of being filled with the grace of your blessed Son, to be holy as he is holy.

—Pope John Paul II[155]

To be holy as Jesus is holy, right from the start: this is an astonishing fact of Mary's life. Does this insight change the way you approach Mary? What does her holiness mean for you as you meditate on her immaculate conception?

- *The United States Catechism for Adults* says, "In the course of time, the doctrine of the Immaculate Conception became more precisely enunciated, as its truth—long supported by the universal popular devotion of the faithful—was better understood by deepening theological inquiry."[156]

  Does it surprise you that our understanding of our faith, as a Church, grows over time? The essentials of the faith are set, but theological inquiry is ongoing, leading to such life-giving dogmas as the Immaculate Conception. Ask the Holy Spirit to help you grow in your appreciation for the robust yet faithful intellectual heritage of the Church.

Pray

Lord, the doctrine of the Immaculate Conception of Mary is both miraculous and disarmingly straightforward. Thank you, Lord, for giving us a faith that is grounded in reason and for reason that is strengthened by faith.

December 9

ST. JUAN DIEGO CUAUHTLATOATZIN (1474–1548)

A visionary, the first indigenous saint of the Americas; patron of indigenous people

and December 12

OUR LADY OF GUADALUPE

Juan Diego's given name was Cuauhtlatoatzin, which means "eagle who speaks." This holy man walked eighteen miles every Sunday to get to Mass. On December 9, 1531, something extraordinary happened during that walk, as he crossed over a hill called Tepeyac: a voice, singing, a brilliant light.

A woman called to the man, familiarly, maternally: "Juanito, Juan Dieguito." The Blessed Mother then appeared and asked him to relay a message to the bishop of Mexico City: she wanted a church built on the hill.

Diego had a hard time convincing the bishop, who asked for proof that the apparition was real. Juan returned to Tepeyac and explained his failure to Mary. She told him to return the next day to gather proof. Juan was delayed the next day, however, when he stayed home to care for his ailing uncle. The day after that, as he sought a priest for his uncle, Mary appeared again. Diego explained why he had missed their appointed meeting, and Mary gently said, "Do not fear any illness or vexation, anxiety or pain. Am I not here who am your Mother? Are you not under my shadow and protection?"[157]

Mary promised that his uncle would be well, and then she instructed Juan to gather and deliver to the bishop roses—which were growing miraculously, out of season, on Tepeyac. Juan obeyed. Later, as the roses tumbled from his tilma, he and the bishop saw another miracle: an image of Mary on the interior of the cloak.

The small church built on Tepeyac has since become the Basilica of Our Lady of Guadalupe. The tilma, with its miraculously imprinted portrait of Mary, is enshrined there. Juan Diego reminds us that the answer to this simple question—"Am

I not here who am your Mother?"—can sustain and calm us by turning our hearts to Mary as we face our struggles.

- When was the last time you worried and stressed over something, only later realizing that you could place it in the capable hands of the one who is your mother?

Like Jesus, Mary is close to all her sons and daughters; as a concerned mother, she accompanies them on their way through life. She shares all the joys and hopes, the sorrows and troubles of God's People, which is made up of men and women of every race and nation.

When the image of the Virgin appeared on the tilma of Juan Diego, it was the prophecy of an embrace: Mary's embrace of all the peoples of the vast expanses of America—the peoples who already lived there, and those who were yet to come.

—Pope Francis[158]

December 13

ST. LUCY (C. 283-304)

Martyr during the Diocletian persecution;
patron saint of the blind, ophthalmologists,
those with eye diseases or conditions, martyrs,
throat infections, the poor, lighters of street lamps

Luminous: that's St. Lucy, also known as St. Lucia, whose name means "light." Halfway through the season of Advent, she reminds us of the most brilliant light, that of Christ.

Lucia's story—her love for Christ and her martyrdom—led to numerous legends but what we know to be true is this: she had complete and utter devotion to God, would not forsake her faith, and was willing to die for it. She has been venerated for centuries and her name is included, with other martyrs, in the canon of the Mass in Eucharistic Prayer I.

To celebrate this beloved saint of light, a Scandinavian tradition dictates that the oldest daughter in a family don a white garment with a red sash, wear a candle-lit wreath of greenery on her head, and wake the family for coffee and pastries. Less risky versions of this tradition still bring delight to girls everywhere. In our family, we voted to have multiple St. Lucias on the feast day, thus saving ourselves from unsaintly sibling squabbles; the lighted candles adorned the pastry, rather than a child's head.

- Whether a saint's story is told through fantastic legends or a quiet chronicle of a steady walk with God, the conclusion is the same: Christ is worth every sacrifice. If someone wrote your story, would it be a fantastic tale or a quiet one? In the end, what matters is not how dramatic our stories are, but that they end with Jesus. Today, ask St. Lucy to light your way as you continue walking toward Christ.

Relying on your goodness, O God, we humbly ask you, by the intercession of your servant, St. Lucy, to give perfect vision to our eyes, that they may serve for your greater honor and glory.

And we pray for the salvation of our souls in this world, that we may come to the enjoyment of the unfailing light of the Lamb of God in heaven.

—Traditional prayer in honor of St. Lucy[159]

December 25

SOLEMNITY OF THE NATIVITY OF THE LORD (CHRISTMAS)

Connect

For to us a child is born,
to us a son is given;
and the government will be upon his shoulder,
and his name will be called
"Wonderful Counselor, Mighty God,
Everlasting Father, Prince of Peace." (Isaiah 9:6, RSVCE)

"Merry Christmas!"
I've had many different kinds of Christmases in my life. When I was growing up, my family had delightful Santa-filled Christmas mornings and turkey dinners with all the trimmings in the afternoon. After my Baptism, the meaning of Christmas obviously took on a new meaning, and one of my delights was diving into Scriptures such as Isaiah's prophetic words.

Later, as a Catholic, going to Mass added new richness to my Christmas celebration. With our children, my husband and I learned to center our Christmas observance around the birth of Christ. We maintained and passed on fun and meaningful traditions we'd grown up with, and we added new and joyful faith-related practices.

And so I've come to recognize that the greeting "Merry Christmas," though it resounds with joy, doesn't begin to capture the glory of this day. Pope Francis, at Midnight Mass in 2020, tapped into the ineffable miracle of the Incarnation:

> *To us a son is given.* Parents of little children know how much love and patience they require. We have to feed them, look after them, bathe them and care for their vulnerability and their needs, which are often difficult to understand. A child makes us feel loved but can also teach us how to love. God was born a child in order to encourage us to care for others. His quiet tears make us realize the uselessness of our many impatient outbursts; and we have so many of them! His disarming love reminds us that our time is not to be spent in feeling sorry for ourselves, but in comforting the tears of the suffering. God came among us in poverty and need, to tell us that in serving the poor, we will show our love for him. From this night onward, as a poet wrote, "God's residence is next to mine, his furniture is love" (Emily Dickinson, *Poems,* XVII).[160]

This Christmas let the Prince of Peace, who can teach us how to care for others, take up residence in your soul and furnish it with his disarming love.

To Ponder or Do

- Top off your Advent journal with a reflection on your most significant insight this season. Did it come from your Advent reading? Was it a lightbulb moment when you were in your newly claimed prayer spot? Were you happy just to slow down a little this year? Whatever it is, capture the moment so that you can remember and savor it.

- Think about how you want to celebrate the Octave of Christmas—Christmas Day through January 1—and the Twelve Days of Christmas. Realistically, most of us can't celebrate for twelve days; pesky things like work and school get in the way. But there's plenty we can do to keep the celebratory spirit alive: Keep the tree and your decorations up until Epiphany, and consider having another small gift exchange on that day. Host a Twelfth Night party. Assemble gingerbread houses. Deliberately save certain activities for this time period. For example, if the weeks leading up to Christmas were too busy for baking with the family, the Twelve Days are the perfect time for kitchen togetherness. Tap into your rebel spirit, and remind the world that the Twelve Days of Christmas don't end on December 25. They are just beginning!

- Did you know you can thank St. Francis of Assisi for your nativity set? Francis had an intense devotion to

Christmas. He told a friend,

I wish to enact the memory of that babe who was born in Bethlehem: to see as much as is possible with my own bodily eyes the discomfort of his infant needs, how he lay in a manger, and how, with an ox and a donkey standing by, he rested on hay.[161]

In the small town of Greccio, Italy, Francis created the first living nativity scene, complete with live animals and a manger. Thank St. Francis for inspiring this powerful and lasting visual reminder.

- Meditate on God's greatness, power, and goodness with these words from Pope Benedict XVI:

God is so great that he can become small. God is so powerful that he can make himself vulnerable and come to us as a defenseless child, so that we can love him. God is so good that he can give up his divine splendor and come down to a stable, so that we might find him, so that his goodness might touch us, give itself to us and continue to work through us. This is Christmas: "You are my son, this day I have begotten you." God has become one of us, so that we can be with him and become like him. As a sign, he chose the Child lying in the manger: this is how God is. This is how we come to know him.[162]

Pray

Lord, thank you for the Incarnation: an unbelievable, improbable, and unpredictable act of your grace. I am reminded on this day that you are the pinnacle of every celebration. As St. Catherine of Siena said, "You are a fire that takes away the coldness, illuminates the mind with its light, and causes me to know your truth. And I know that you are beauty and wisdom itself. The food of angels, you gave yourself to man in the fire of your love."[163]

December 26

ST. STEPHEN, THE FIRST MARTYR

Connect

The Acts of the Apostles is our only source for what we know of St. Stephen, the first Christian martyr (protomartyr). He was one of seven men the disciples chose to act as deacons and care for the needs of widows. Described as "filled with faith and the holy Spirit" as well as "grace and power," he was "working great wonders and signs among the people" (Acts 6:5, 8).

Stephen's power as a preacher and his eloquent evangelization about Jesus as the Messiah earned him enemies, and he was arrested on charges of blasphemy. He was stoned to death, with "a young man named Saul" looking on in approval (Acts 7:58). As he was dying, Stephen cried out, "Lord, do not hold this sin against them" (7:60), beautifully echoing the words of Jesus,

"Father, forgive them, they know not what they do" (Luke 23:34).

Stephen's faith was powerful, and his forgiveness of his enemies complete, immediate, and Christlike. We may never face the deadly persecution that Stephen faced, but we can ask ourselves these questions: Whom do I need to forgive? Do I truly believe that my enemies don't know what they're doing? Can I bring myself to pray for them, and can I ask for the grace to forgive them?

To Ponder or Do

- Read Stephen's story in chapters 6 and 7 of the Acts of the Apostles. What part of Stephen's story hits you at the deepest level?

- The day after Christmas is a feast day, a day of joy, and one of the Twelve Days of Christmas. It's not easy to divert our attention from our celebrations to something as serious as the martyrdom of Stephen, yet the Church has chosen this day to honor the first man to die for Christ. Why do you think that is? Take a moment today to ask Stephen to pray for an increase in faith, in yourself and in the world, that we may all be able to ask God to forgive our enemies with as much conviction as Stephen did.

- In England St. Stephen's Day is known as Boxing Day. The name comes from a tradition of saving money throughout the year in a box and then breaking the box open after Christmas and giving alms to the poor. Some strands of the tradition have the gifts going to servants and tradespeople. Consider giving a gift, either monetary or clothing or other goods, to a charity.

Pray

Heavenly Father, St. Stephen was a beautiful example of Christian selflessness and charity. His love for others extended to all, from the widows he served to the authorities who unjustly accused him of sacrilege and blasphemy and who ultimately murdered him. Help me have a spirit and a heart like Stephen's, to be "filled with faith and the holy Spirit" and full of "grace and power" (Acts 6:5, 8). Amen.

December 27

ST. JOHN THE APOSTLE AND EVANGELIST

Connect

John, one of the first apostles called by Jesus, is the author of the Gospel of John, the Book of Revelation, and three New Testament epistles, although scholars debate exactly

what John penned and what his followers may have written. However the scholarship shakes out, it is undisputed that
John's Gospel is uniquely beautiful, opening as it does with
these gripping words:

> In the beginning was the Word,
>   and the Word was with God,
>   and the Word was God. (1:1)

Often referred to as part of Jesus' inner circle, John was
present with James and Peter at the Transfiguration, was the
one to whom Jesus entrusted his mother at the crucifixion,
and was the first, after Mary of Magdala, to run to the empty
tomb. His Gospel identifies him as "the disciple whom Jesus
loved" (see John 13:23; 19:26; 20:2; 21:20).

Jesus referred to John and his brother, James, as the "sons of
thunder," coincidentally revealing the delightful fact that Jesus
nicknamed his friends. We don't know why he dubbed James
and John "Boanerges" ("sons of thunder"; Mark 3:17), but we
can guess that it had something to do with strong, impulsive
personalities and the audacity to say such things as "Teacher,
we want you to do for us whatever we ask of you. . . . Grant
that in your glory we may sit one at your right and the other
at your left" (10:35, 37).

Jesus set the two men straight on what, precisely, they were
proposing. I wonder if he shook his head and rolled his eyes.
Or did he nickname them in that moment?

Perhaps the nickname arose when Jesus and his disciples
approached a Samaritan village and were turned away (see

Luke 9:51-56). James and John were admirably eager but too zealous, asking, "Lord, do you want us to call down fire from heaven to consume them" (9:54)? "Umm, no, guys," Jesus said. "Let's just go to another village."

It's comforting and wonderful that Scripture paints a picture of the apostles that includes their folly and flaws. John was imperfect, yet Jesus invited him into his inner circle. John's identity as the disciple Jesus loved should give modern-day disciples like us great hope in the saving love of Christ.

To Ponder or Do

- Nicknames often indicate friendship and affection. Do you picture Jesus as someone who would offer a nickname to his followers? If Jesus were to nickname you, what would that nickname be?

- In John 13:23-26, John is the beloved disciple who is reclining next to Jesus. Jesus, John, and Simon Peter share an intimate moment of conversation about who will betray Jesus. If it's hard to imagine whispering secrets to Jesus, consider the fact that we do this every time we pray. We can be "reclining at Jesus' side" (13:23) as we speak to him. What do you want to tell him about what you're experiencing this Christmas season?

- John's Gospel differs in style from the synoptic Gospels of Matthew, Mark, and Luke, and thus it offers another perspective on the life, death, and resurrection of the Lord. Do you have a favorite Gospel? If you haven't read through the entire Gospel of John, consider setting aside a little time during the Twelve Days to dip further into it and see what you think of its tone and flavor.

- There's a legend that John was served poisoned wine and survived; out of that legend grew a tradition of blessing and serving wine on his feast day. Raise a glass to St. John today, and celebrate his immense love for our Lord.

Pray

Lord, each of your apostles was different, each was imperfect, and each one loved you with a heart and devotion unique to the apostle. Help me see my unique personality, recognize my flaws, and acknowledge the gifts and challenges that would earn me a nickname from you. Help me be a beloved disciple. St. John the Divine, son of thunder, pray for me!

December 28

FEAST OF THE HOLY INNOCENTS

Connect

Today is another feast day that gives us pause amid the revelry and joy of the Christmas season, a pause worth taking.

It is also a timely, beautiful reminder that our faith never fully separates the cradle from the cross: the human condition will always include suffering and the need for our Savior.

Enraged that the wise men chose not to return to him and report on the whereabouts of the baby Jesus, Herod took action. Motivated by his thirst for power, he ordered the slaughter of all male children two years old and younger in and around Bethlehem. Today we honor those innocent victims of his brutal tyranny.

On this feast, pause and think about the fear St. Joseph must have felt as he fled with Jesus and Mary and did everything he could to protect his family. May these martyrs, the Holy Innocents, pray for our world today.

To Ponder or Do

- Read Matthew 2.

A voice was heard in Ramah,
wailing and loud lamentation,
Rachel weeping for her children;
she refused to be consoled,
because they were no more.
(Matthew 2:18, RSVCE)

Today pray for all victims of violence and for all parents who have lost children to violence, crime, drug abuse, and other contemporary scourges.

- Pray for mothers and fathers who choose abortion: for those who cannot be consoled after that heartbreaking choice and for those who have hardened their hearts to what their choices mean.

- In his 2016 letter to the bishops on the feast of the Holy Innocents, Pope Francis wrote,

Christian joy does not arise on the fringes of reality, by ignoring it or acting as if it did not exist. Christian joy is born from a call—the same call that St. Joseph received—to embrace and protect human life, especially that of the holy innocents of our own day. Christmas is a time that challenges us to protect life, to help it be born and grow.[164]

How do you answer the call to embrace and protect human life and help human life grow?

Pray

Lord, help me listen to your call and embrace and protect human life, to "help it be born and grow" in every way. Help me do all I can to care for the spiritual and material needs of others, from their conception to natural death. Amen.

December 29–31

FIFTH, SIXTH, AND SEVENTH DAYS OF CHRISTMAS

We're still in the Octave of Christmas! The first eight days of Christmas, from December 25 to January 1, are called the Octave of Christmas, and each day is a solemnity—the highest form of feast—and a cause for celebration. Just as we celebrated Easter for an eight-day octave, we observe the joy of Christmas for an extended period. What will you do during this time of celebration?

- Haven't sent out Christmas cards yet? No problem. It's still Christmas.

- Didn't bake Christmas cookies early in December? Christmas is still here, so get started.

- Fretting that you're late with a gift you meant to give a friend? We're still in the middle of this gift-giving season.

- That caroling session didn't happen? Schedule it now.

- No time before Christmas to watch your favorite Christmas movies? You know what to do.

It's hard to "swim upstream" in a society that wants to pack up Christmas on December 26, but it's a swim worth taking. Christmas joy is meant to last for days and days. Don't waste a minute of that joy.

Happy Octave, Happy Twelve Days, Happy Christmas!

Wrapping Up . . . or Not?

Wait, is that it? We've reached the end? The year is over? No, there's never really an end to liturgical living. There is always another beginning. The path is an ever-widening spiral.

The beauty of the liturgical calendar is that, like the circular, predictable rhythms of the seasons, we will circle back to what's known and familiar. And God will make something new of us each year.

Grow from the fasts, relish the feasts, and ask the saints—there's one waiting to hear from you every day—to pray for you. May the liturgical year be your companion this year and always.

Acknowledgments

Many thanks to Beth McNamara, Jessica Montgomery, and Lucy Scholand, who helped to shape this book. I'm so grateful to Suzanne Earl for the beautiful design. And immense gratitude to Cindy Cavnar—more than an editor, she is, to my endless personal and spiritual benefit, a friend.

Notes

1. St. Ambrose of Milan, *The Virgin*, bk. 2, chap. 2, no. 7, in Philip Schaff and Henry Wace, eds., *Ambrose: Selected Works and Letters*, vol. 10, *The Nicene and Post-Nicene Fathers, Series 2*, https://www.newadvent.org/fathers/34072.htm.

2. https://setonshrine.org/wp-content/uploads/2020/03/St-Elizabeth-Ann-Seton-Quotes.pdf, from *Collected Writings*, vol. 1, page 245.

3. Pope Francis, Angelus, Feast of the Baptism of the Lord, January 12, 2020, https://www.vatican.va/content/francesco/en/angelus/2020/documents/papa-francesco_angelus_20200112.html.

4. Pope Paul VI, *Evangelii Nuntiandi* [On Evangelization in the Modern World], December 8, 1975, 80, https://www.vatican.va/content/paul-vi/en/apost_exhortations/documents/hf_p-vi_exh_19751208_evangelii-nuntiandi.html.

5. Quoted by Margaret E. Ayala, "St. Francis de Sales: 'Have Patience with All Things,'" https://www.oblates.org/updates/st-francis-de-sales-have-patience-with-all-things.

6. Msgr. Robert Hugh Benson, quoted in John Chapin, ed., *The Book of Catholic Quotations* (New York, NY: Farrar, Straus and Cudahy, 1956), 219.

7. St. Frances de Sales, as quoted in Jill Haak Adels, *The Wisdom of the Saints: An Anthology* (New York, NY: Oxford University Press, 1987), 124.

8. *Catholic Digest*, February 1, 2021, "St. Brigid of Kildare--I Would Like an Abundance of Peace . . . " https://www.catholicdigest.com/from-the-magazine/quiet-moment/st-brigid-of-kildare-i-would-like-an-abundance-of-peace/.

9. Quoted by Fr. Antonio Spadaro, "Interview with Pope Francis," August 19, 2013, https://www.vatican.va/content/francesco/en/speeches/2013/september/documents/papa-francesco_20130921_intervista-spadaro.html.

10. Pope John Paul II, "Cappella Papale for the Canonization of 123 New Saints," October 1, 2000, 5, https://www.vatican.va/content/john-paul-ii/en/homilies/2000/documents/hf_jp-ii_hom_20001001_canonization.html.

11. Quoted in Vatican News, "Josephine Bakhita (1869–1947)," https://www.vatican.va/news_services/liturgy/saints/ns_lit_doc_20001001_giuseppina-bakhita_en.html.

12. Pope Gregory I, *Dialogus*, book 2, chap. 33, https://www.osb.org/gen/greg.

13. Pope Gregory I, *Dialogus.*

14. Pope Gregory I, *Dialogus.*

15. Pope Gregory I, *Dialogus.*

16. "Chair of Peter," *Catholic Encyclopedia,* https://www.newadvent.org/cathen/03551e.htm.

17. St. Gregory of Narek, *Book of Lamentations,* 3:2–3, http://212.34.228.170/narek_new/t1_3.htm.

18. Michael Papazian in an interview with Mike Aquilina, "The Ancient Wisdom of Armenia's 'Doctor of Mercy' for the New Decade," January 9, 2020, *Angelus*, https://angelusnews.com/faith/a-new-book-introduces-us-to-the-most-important-saint-you-never-heard-of/.

19. St. Gregory of Narek, *Tenets of Prayer,* prayer 10, stanza D, https://www.stgregoryofnarek.am/book.php?parent_id=11&type=2&type_1=none.

20. Pope Francis, Apostolic Letter *Patris Corde* [With a Father's Heart], https://www.vatican.va/content/francesco/en/apost_letters/documents/papa-francesco-lettera-ap_20201208_patris-corde.html.

21. Rev. John A. Tolton, as quoted by David O'Reilly, "Mother Katharine Drexel to Be Canonized Today," *The Baltimore Sun,* October 1, 2000, https://www.baltimoresun.com/news/bs-xpm-2000-10-01-0009300099-story.html.

22. Quoted in Carol Kelly-Gangi, *365 Days with the Saints: A Year of Wisdom from the Saints* (New York, NY: Wellfleet Press, 2015), 42.

23. "Daily, Daily Sing to Mary," trans. Henry Bittleston, https://hymnary.org/text/daily_daily_sing_to_mary.

24. *The Passion of the Holy Martyrs Perpetua and Felicity,* trans. R.E. Wallis, chap. 1, in Alexander Roberts, James Donaldson, A. Cleveland Coxe, eds., *Ante-Nicene Fathers,* vol. 3, https://www. newadvent.org/fathers/0324.htm; single paragraph in original.

25. *The Passion of the Holy Martyrs Perpetua and Felicity,* chap. 1.

26. St. John of God, quoted by Mike Eisenbath, "Here's Why I Think St. John of God Should Be a New Patron for the Mentally Ill," *Aleteia,* May 10, 2017, https://aleteia.org/2017/05/10/heres-why-i-think-st-john-of-god-should-be-a-new-patron-for-the-mentally-ill/.

27. Quoted by Claire Dwyer, "A Woman for All Seasons: St. Frances of Rome," https://spiritualdirection. com/2019/03/09/a-woman-for-all-seasons-st-frances-of-rome.

28. Bieler, L, *The Works of St. Patrick, St. Secundinus, Hymn of St. Patrick* [*Ancient Christian Writers* 17], (Westminster, MD: Newman Press, 1953), 25.

29. *Confession of St. Patrick* (Grand Rapids, MI: Christian Classics Ethereal Library), 5:16, https://archive.org/stream/ ConfessionOfStPatrick/Confession%20of%20St%20Patrick_djvu. txt.

30. *Confession of St. Patrick* (Grand Rapids, MI: Christian Classics Ethereal Library), 7:23.

31. *Irish Central Staff,* July 13, 2021, "St. Patrick's Breastplate: The Prayer of Ireland's Patron Saint," https://www.irishcentral.com/roots/ st-patricks-breastplate-prayer-irelands-patron-saint.

32. Pope John Paul II, General Audience, September 10, 1997, 4, https:// www.vatican.va/content/john-paul-ii/en/audiences/1997/documents/ hf_jp-ii_aud_10091997.html.

33. See United States Conference of Catholic Bishops, "Fast & Abstinence," https://www.usccb.org/prayer-and-worship/liturgical-year-and-calendar/lent/ catholic-information-on-lenten-fast-and-abstinence.

34. Message of His Holiness Pope Francis for Lent 2018, November 1, 2017, https://www.vatican.va/content/francesco/en/messages/lent/ documents/papa-francesco_20171101_messaggio-quaresima2018. html.

35. Message of His Holiness Benedict XVI for Lent 2013, October 15, 2012, 3, 4, https://www.vatican.va/content/benedict-xvi/en/messages/lent/documents/hf_ben-xvi_mes_20121015_lent-2013.html.

36. St. Augustine, in Phillip Schaff, *The Confessions and Letters of St. Augustine with a Sketch of His Life and Work,* chap. 4, 9, https://www.ccel.org/ccel/schaff/npnf101.vi.VIII.IV.html.

37. Pope Francis, Homily of Palm Sunday of the Passion of the Lord, St. Peter's Basilica, March 28, 2021, https://www.vatican.va/content/francesco/en/homilies/2021/documents/papa-francesco_20210328_omelia-palme.html; single paragraph in original.

38. *Crossroads Initiative*, "Palm Sunday: He Comes in Humility—Andrew of Crete," https://www.crossroadsinitiative.com/media/articles/palmsundayhecomesinhumility/.

39. St. Francisca Salesia Aviat, quoted in Kelly-Gangi, 9.

40. Pope John Paul II, Homily for the Canonization of Sr. Mary Faustina Kowalska, April 30, 2000, 6, https://www.vatican.va/content/john-paul-ii/en/homilies/2000/documents/hf_jp-ii_hom_20000430_faustina.html.

41. Pope Francis, Homily on the Solemnity of Pentecost, May 23, 2021, https://www.vatican.va/content/francesco/it/homilies/2021/documents/papa-francesco_20210523_omelia-pentecoste.html.

42. From letters of St. Francis of Paolo, quoted in Pontifical University St. Thomas Aquinas, "Turn to the Lord with a Pure Heart," https://www.vatican.va/spirit/documents/spirit_20010402_francesco-paola_en.html.

43. St. Bernadette, quoted in John Lochran, *The Miracle of Lourdes: A Message of Healing and Hope* (Cincinnati, OH: St. Anthony Messenger Press, 2008), 39.

44. Lochran, 130.

45. Pope Francis, Apostolic Exhortation *Evangelii Gaudium* [The Joy of the Gospel], November 24, 2013, 266, https://www.vatican.va/content/francesco/en/apost_exhortations/documents/papa-francesco_esortazione-ap_20131124_evangelii-gaudium.html.

46. St. Augustine, quoted in Adels, 125.

47. Pope John Paul II, Homily for the Canonization of Six New Saints, May 16, 2004, 7, https://www.vatican.va/content/john-paul-ii/en/homilies/2004/documents/hf_jp-ii_hom_20040516_canonizations.html.

48. St. Gianna Molla, quoted in "Gianna Beretta Molla (1922–1962)," https://www.vatican.va/news_services/liturgy/saints/ns_lit_doc_20040516_beretta-molla_en.html.

49. Pope Benedict XVI, General Audience, November 24, 2010, https://www.vatican.va/content/benedict-xvi/en/audiences/2010/documents/hf_ben-xvi_aud_20101124.html.

50. Catherine of Siena, quoted in Sigrid Undset, *Catherine of Siena* (San Francisco, CA: Ignatius Press, 2009), 317.

51. Pope John Paul II, Apostolic Exhortation *Redemptoris Custos* [Guardian of the Redeemer], August 15, 1989, 22, https://www.vatican.va/content/john-paul-ii/en/apost_exhortations/documents/hf_jp-ii_exh_15081989_redemptoris-custos.html.

52. Pope Pius X, Prayer to Saint Joseph the Worker, https://catholictruth.net/CTNet_RC/en/archive.asp?d=20150314P.

53. Pope Francis, Angelus, September 27, 2020, https://www.vatican.va/content/francesco/en/angelus/2020/documents/papa-francesco_angelus_20200927.html.

54.   From Prayer of Pope Francis at the Shrine of Our Lady of Fatima, May 12, 2017, https://www.vatican.va/content/francesco/en/prayers/documents/papa-francesco_preghiere_20170512_fatima.html.

55. Prayer to St. Rita, https://www.daily-prayers.org/angels-and-saints/prayers-to-saint-rita-of-cascia/.

56. Loyola Press, "Saint Bede the Venerable," https://www.loyolapress.com/catholic-resources/saints/saints-stories-for-all-ages/saint-bede-the-venerable/.

57. Fr. Pietro Giacomo Bacci, *The Life of St. Philip Neri,* ed. Frederick Ignatius Antrobus (London: Kegan Paul, Trench, Trubner, 1902), vol. 1, 191–192, https://www.google.com/books/edition/The_Life_of_Saint_Philip_Neri/hzQtAAAAMAAJ?hl=en&gbpv=1&bsq=merry%20.

58. Pope Francis, Message on the Fifth Centenary of the Birth of St. Philip Neri, May 26, 2015, http://www.totus2us.com/vocation/saints/st-philip-neri/.

59. Quoted by Pope John Paul II on the Occasion of the Fourth Centenary of the Death of St. Philip Neri, https://www.vatican.va/content/john-paul-ii/en/letters/1994/documents/hf_jp-ii_let_07101994_filippo-neri.html.

60. See W.P Barrett, trans.,

The Trial of Joan of Arc (Gotham House, 1932), 115, https://sourcebooks.fordham.edu/basis/joanofarc-trial.asp.

61. Pope Benedict XVI, General Audience, January 26, 2011, https://www.vatican.va/content/benedict-xvi/en/audiences/2011/documents/hf_ben-xvi_aud_20110126.html.

62. Quoted in Dwayne E. Pickels, *Joan of Arc* (Philadelphia, PA: Chelsea House, 2002), 26, https://www.google.com/books/edition/Joan_of_Arc/wZaPMMiyKoYC?hl=en&gbpv=1&bsq=I%20do%20not%20fear%20the%20soldiers%20.

63. Joan of Arc, quoted by Pope Benedict XVI, January 26, 2011.

64. Pope John Paul II, General Audience, October 2, 1996, 1, 2, https://www.vatican.va/content/john-paul-ii/it/audiences/1996/documents/hf_jp-ii_aud_19961002.html.

65. St. Margaret Mary, "12 Promises of the Sacred Heart," https://www.ewtn.com/catholicism/library/12-promises-of-the-sacred-heart-13683.

66. See, for example, Fordham University, https://sourcebooks.fordham.edu/basis/willibald-boniface.asp.

67. St. Boniface, quoted in Adels, 83.

68. Pope Benedict XVI, General Audience, November 28, 2007, https://www.vatican.va/content/benedict-xvi/en/audiences/2007/documents/hf_ben-xvi_aud_20071128.html.

69. Pope Benedict XV, Encyclical *Principi Apostolorum Petro* [To Peter the Prince of the Apostles], citing John 5:35, October 5, 1920, 11, https://www.vatican.va/content/benedict-xv/en/encyclicals/documents/hf_ben-xv_enc_05101920_principi-apostolorum-petro.html.

70. St. Ephrem, quoted in Pope John Paul II, General Audience, February 5, 2003, 4, https://www.vatican.va/content/john-paul-ii/en/audiences/2003/documents/hf_jp-ii_aud_20030205.html.

71. St. Ephrem, hymn *De Fide*, quoted by Pope Benedict XVI, General Audience, November 28, 2007, https://www.vatican.va/content/benedict-xvi/en/audiences/2007/documents/hf_ben-xvi_aud_20071128.html.

72. St. Anthony of Padua, St. Anthony of Padua, *The Sermons of St. Antony of Padua*, Paul Spilsbury, trans. (from the Critical Latin Edition of the *Centro Studi Antoniani*, Padova, Italia, 1979, "The Fifteenth Sunday after Pentecost," Prologue, 5.

73. Anthony of Padua, quoted in Martin H. Manser, *The Westminster Collection of Christian Quotations* (Louisville, KY: Westminster John Knox Press, 2001), 10.

74. John Chapin, ed., *The Book of Catholic Quotations* (New York, NY: Farrar, Strauss and Cudahy, 1956), 932.

75. Pope Paul VI, Apostolic Exhortation *Evangelii Nuntiandi*, 80.

76. Pope Francis, Homily for the Holy Mass and Blessing of the Sacred Pallium for the New Metropolitan Archbishops on the Solemnity of Saints Peter and Paul, Apostles, June 29, 2021, https://www.vatican.va/content/francesco/en/homilies/2021/documents/papa-francesco_20210629_omelia-pallio.html.

77. St. Benedict, quoted in Kelly-Gangi, 86.

78. St. Bonaventure, quoted in Chapin, 561.

79. St. Thérèse of Lisieux, quoted in Kelly-Gangi, 138.

80. St. Thérèse of Lisieux, quoted in Kelly-Gangi, 141.

81. Fr. Stanley Rother, as quoted in *Catholic News Agency*, "Father Stanley Rother: The First U.S.-born Martyr," posted at Archdiocese of San Antonio, https://www.archsa.org/blog/father-stanley-rother-the-first-u.s.-born-martyr.

82. Fr. Stanley Rother, quoted in María Ruiz Scaperlanda, *The Shepherd Who Didn't Run: Fr. Stanley Rother, Martyr from Oklahoma* (Huntington, IN: Our Sunday Visitor, 2015), 186.

83. St. Ignatius of Loyola, *Suscipe,* https://www.loyolapress.com/catholic-resources/prayer/traditional-catholic-prayers/saints-prayers/suscipe-prayer-saint-ignatius-of-loyola/.

84. Pope Francis, Angelus, February 28, 2021, https://www.vatican.va/content/francesco/en/angelus/2021/documents/papa-francesco_angelus_20210228.html.

85. "Teresa Benedict of the Cross Edith Stein (1891-1942)," https://www.vatican.va/news_services/liturgy/saints/ns_lit_doc_19981011_edith_stein_en.html.

86. "Teresa Benedict of the Cross Edith Stein."

87. St. Teresa Benedict of the Cross, quoted in *Catholic Culture*, Freda Mary Oben, "Let Us Go for Our People," https://www.catholicculture.org/culture/library/view.cfm?recnum=567.

88. Quoted in Cindy Cavnar, *The Saints from A to Z: An Inspirational Dictionary* (Ann Arbor, MI: Charis Books, 2000), 189.

89. Pope John Paul II, quoted in "Teresa Benedict of the Cross Edith Stein," https://www.vatican.va/news_services/liturgy/saints/ns_lit_doc_19981011_edith_stein_en.html.

90. "Teresa Benedict of the Cross."

91. Catholic Online, "St. Jane Frances de Chantal," https://www.catholic.org/saints/saint.php?saint_id=60.

92. St. Vincent de Paul, quoted from *Butler's Lives of the Saints*, in Chris Sparks, "In Darkness, Light," https://www.thedivinemercy.org/articles/darkness-light.

93. Quoted in "Wisdom from St. Jane de Chantal," https://www.oblates.org/st-jane-wisdom.

94. Pope John Paul II, Homily at the Canonization Mass of St. Maximilan Kolbe, quoted at https://catholicexchange.com/the-patron-saint-for-a-difficult-century-st-maximilian-kolbe.

95. Cavnar, 110.

96. St. Maximilian Kolbe, quoted by Pope Benedict XVI, General Audience, August 13, 2008, https://www.vatican.va/content/benedict-xvi/en/audiences/2008/documents/hf_ben-xvi_aud_20080813.html.

97. Pope Pius XII, *Munificentissimus Deus* [The Most Bountiful God], 7-8, https://www.vatican.va/content/pius-xii/en/apost_constitutions/documents/hf_p-xii_apc_19501101_munificentissimus-deus.html.

98. St. Augustine, *Confessions*, book 1, 1, https://www.newadvent.org/fathers/110101.htm.

99. St. Augustine, book 5, chap. 7, 13, https://www.newadvent.org/fathers/110105.htm.

100. St. Augustine, *Confessions*, trans. Henry Chadwick (Oxford, England: Oxford University Press, 2009), 201.

101. St. Augustine, *Confessions*, book 8, 29.

102. St. Augustine, trans. Chadwick, 201.

103. Pope Gregory the Great, quoted in Adels, 40.

104. Mother Teresa's biography, https://www.vatican.va/news_services/liturgy/saints/ns_lit_doc_20031019_madre-teresa_en.html.

105. Quoted in Christie R. Ritter, *Mother Teresa: Humanitarian and Advocate for the Poor* (Edina, MN: Abdo Publishing, 2011), 51.

106. Pope Paul VI, Apostolic Exhortation *Marialis Cultus* [Marian Devotion], February 2, 1974, 7, https://www.vatican.va/content/paul-vi/en/apost_exhortations/documents/hf_p-vi_exh_19740202_marialis-cultus.html, quoting *Roman Missal,* September 8, Prayer after Communion.

107. Pope Francis, Morning Meditation, "Small and Holy," September 8, 2014, *L'Osservatore Romano,* weekly ed. in English, no. 37, September 12, 2014, https://www.vatican.va/content/francesco/en/cotidie/2014/documents/papa-francesco-cotidie_20140908_small-and-holy.html.

108. Pope Benedict XVI, *Jesus of Nazareth: Holy Week: From the Entrance into Jerusalem to the Resurrection* (San Francisco, CA: Ignatius Press, 2011), 165–166.

109. St. Andrew of Crete, *Exaltatione sanctae crucis, Oratio* 10, posted at https://www.crossroadsinitiative.com/media/articles/triumphandexaltationoftheholycross/.

110. St. Francis' Prayer, quoted at Vatican News, "Feast of the Exaltation of the Holy Cross," https://www.vaticannews.va/en/liturgical-holidays/feast-of-the-exaltation-of-the-holy-cross.html

111. Pope Benedict XVI, Apostolic Letter Proclaiming St. Hildegard a Doctor of the Church, 4, https://www.vatican.va/content/benedict-xvi/en/apost_letters/documents/hf_ben-xvi_apl_20121007_ildegarda-bingen.html.

112. St. Hildegard of Bingen, quoted in Kelly-Gangi, 269.

113. St. Bede, quoted in Adels, 93.

114. Pope Francis, General Audience, April 13, 2016, https://www.vatican.va/content/francesco/it/audiences/2016/documents/papa-francesco_20160413_udienza-generale.html.

115. Pope Francis, Morning Meditation, *L'Osservatore Romano*, weekly ed. in English, no. 27, June 9, 2021, https://www.vatican.va/content/francesco/en/cotidie/2017/documents/papa-francesco-cotidie_20170609_advice-for-the-weekend.html.

116. "The Archangels: Heralds and Our Fellow Servants," wau.org/resources/article/the_archangels.

117. St. Jerome, as quoted in Stuart Squires, "St. Jerome: The Patron of Irascible, Morbidly Sensitive, Old Curmudgeons," https://dailytheology.org/2015/09/30/st-jerome-the-patron-of-irascible-morbidly-sensitive-old-curmudgeons/.

118. St. Jerome, quoted in Chapin, 458.

119. St. Thérèse of Lisieux, *Story of a Soul*, trans. John Clarke (Washington, DC: ICS Publications, 1996), 242-243.

120. St. Thérèse of Lisieux, quoted in Peter Doyle, *Butler's Lives of the Saints: October* (Collegeville, MN: The Liturgical Press, 1997), 4.

121. St. Thérèse of Lisieux, quoted in Adels, 4.

122. Pope Francis, quoted by Gabriella Ceraso, "Pope at Mass: Guardian Angels, Our Daily Gate to the Father," October 2, 2018, https://www.vaticannews.va/en/pope-francis/mass-casa-santa-marta/2018-10/pope-francis-homily-daily-mass-guardian-angels-transcendence.html.

123. St. John Vianney, quoted in Adels, 23.

124. Quoted in Cavnar, 86.

125. St. Mother Théodore Guérin, Sisters of Providence of Saint Mary-of-the-Woods, https://spsmw.org/quotations/at-each-step-we-can-admire/.

126. St. Francis of Assisi, quoted in Christine Valters Paintner, *Illuminating the Way: Embracing the Wisdom of Monks and Mystics* (Notre Dame, IN: Sorin Books, 2016), 2, https://assets.avemariapress.com/media/files/da2c9dbe6727a82dcf030c49966d4978/Illuminating_the_Way_Excerpt.pdf.

127. G. K. Chesterton, *St. Francis of Assisi* (New York: Clydesdale Press, 2020), 5.

128. Doyle, 17.

129. Doyle, 17.

130. Vatican News, "St. Francis of Assis, Founder of the Franciscan Order, Patron of Italy," https://www.vaticannews.va/en/saints/10/04/st--francis-of-assisi--founder-of-the-franciscan--order--patron-.html.

131. Doyle, 22.

132. Pope Francis, *Fratelli Tutti* [All Brothers], 287, https://www.vatican.va/content/francesco/en/encyclicals/documents/papa-francesco_20201003_enciclica-fratelli-tutti.html.

133. Pope John Paul II, Homily for the Canonization of Sr. Mary Faustina Kowalska, 2, April 30, 2000, 2.

134. St. Faustina, *Diary,* 132, as quoted in John Paul II, homily, 2.

135. Bartolo Longo, quoted in Ann M. Brown, *Apostle of the Rosary: Blessed Bartolo Longo* (New Hope Publications, KY: New Hope Publications, 2004), 53.

136. Pope John Paul II, Apostolic Letter *Rosarium Virginis Mariae* [The Rosary of the Virgin Mary], October 16, 2002, 3, https://www.vatican.va/content/john-paul-ii/en/apost_letters/2002/documents/hf_jp-ii_apl_20021016_rosarium-virginis-mariae.html.

137. St. Teresa of Ávila, quoted at https://www.discerninghearts.com/catholic-podcasts/st-teresa-of-avila-quotes/.

138. St. Teresa of Ávila, quoted by Pope Benedict XVI, General Audience, February 2, 2011, https://www.vatican.va/content/benedict-xvi/en/audiences/2011/documents/hf_ben-xvi_aud_20110202.html.

139. Pope Benedict XVI, *Jesus of Nazareth: From the Baptism in the Jordan to the Transfiguration* (New York, NY: Random House, 2007), 208–209.

140. Pope Francis, Angelus, November 1, 2020, https://www.vatican.va/content/francesco/it/angelus/2020/documents/papa-francesco_angelus_20201101.html.

141. Prayer of St. Gertrude: Releasing Souls from Purgatory, https://prayforsouls.org/ways/prayers/st-gertrude.

142. Pope Francis, Angelus, November 1, 2020.

143. C. S. Lewis, *Letters to Malcolm, Chiefly on Prayer,* https://www.angelfire.com/pa3/OldWorldBasic/purgatorycslewis.htm.

144. St. Elizabeth of the Trinity, quoted at https://www.carmelitedcj.org/carmel/saints-of-carmel/160-bl-elizabeth-of-the-trinity.

145. St. Elizabeth of the Trinity, quoted at Discalced Carmelite Nuns of Rochester, https://carmelitesofrochester.org/new-page-82.

146. St. Elizabeth of the Trinity, quoted at https://www.carmelitedcj.org/carmel/saints-of-carmel/160-bl-elizabeth-of-the-trinity.

147. Pope Leo XIII to Mother Cabrini, https://www.mothercabrini.org/who-we-are/our-history/not-to-the-east-but-to-the-west/.

148. Mother Cabrini, "A Discernment Prayer," https://www.mothercabrini.org/spirituality/discernment-resources/.

149. Pope Benedict XVI, General Audience, October 6, 2010, https://www.vatican.va/content/benedict-xvi/en/audiences/2010/documents/hf_ben-xvi_aud_20101006.html.

150. St. Gertrude the Great, quoted by Pope Benedict at General Audience, October 6, 2010.

151. Archbishop William E. Lori, Homily on the Feast of the Presentation of Mary, November 21, 2017, https://www.archbalt.org/archbishop-loris-homily-presentation-blessed-virgin-mary-senior-leadership-retreat-day/.

152. Pope Francis, homily, November 26, 2018, https://www.vaticannews.va/en/pope-francis/mass-casa-santa-marta/2018-11/pope-francis-mass-generosity-enlarges-heart.html.

153. Pope Pius IX, Apostolic Constitution *Ineffabilis Deus* [On the Immaculate Conception], quoting Pope Alexander VII, https://www.newadvent.org/library/docs_pi09id.htm.

154. Frank Sheed, *Theology for Beginners* (London: Sheed & Ward, 2001), 134.

155. Pope John Paul II, Prayer for the Solemnity of the Immaculate Conception, December 8, 1998, 2, https://www.vatican.va/content/john-paul-ii/en/speeches/1998/december/documents/hf_jp-ii_spe_08121998_prayer-Maria.html.

156. *The United States Catechism for Adults,* (Washington, DC: USCCB, 2006), 143–144.

157. See Br. Michael, "Our Lady of Guadalupe," June 10, 2004, https://catholicism.org/brmichael-guadalupe.html.

158. Pope Francis, General Audience, December 11, 2013, https://www.vatican.va/content/francesco/en/audiences/2013/documents/papa-francesco_20131211_udienza-generale.html.

159. Carol Kelly-Gangi, 365 Days with the Saints: *A Year of Wisdom from the Saints* (New York, NY: Wellfleet Press, 2015), 265.

160. Pope Francis, Midnight Mass Homily on the Solemnity of the Nativity of the Lord, December 24, 2020, https://www.vatican.va/content/francesco/en/homilies/2020/documents/papa-francesco_20201224_omelia-natale.html.

161. Quoted in *Aleteia*, Bret Thomas, "St. Francis' Reenactment of Christmas Was the First Nativity Scene," December 16, 2020, https://aleteia.org/2020/12/16/st-francis-reenactment-of-christmas-was-the-first-nativity-scene/.

162. Pope Benedict XVI, Midnight Mass Homily on the Solemnity of the Nativity of the Lord, December 24, 2005, https://www.vatican.va/content/benedict-xvi/en/homilies/2005/documents/hf_ben-xvi_hom_20051224_christmas.html.

163. St. Catherine of Siena, quoted in Adels, 184.

164. Letter of Pope Francis to Bishops on the Feast of the Holy Innocents, December 28, 2016, https://www.vatican.va/content/francesco/en/letters/2016/documents/papa-francesco_20161228_santi-innocenti.html.